Perils and Possibilities

Perils and Possibilities

Social Activism and the Law

Byron M. Sheldrick

Fernwood Publishing • Halifax, Nova Scotia

Editing: Jane Butler
Cover photo (top): Tony Sukaroff
Design and production: Beverley Rach
Printed and bound in Canada by: Hignell Printing Limited

A publication of:
Fernwood Publishing
Site 2A, Box 5, 8422 St. Margaret's Bay Road
Black Point, Nova Scotia, B0J 1B0
and 324 Clare Avenue
Winnipeg, Manitoba, R3L 1S3
www.fernwoodbooks.ca

Fernwood Publishing Company Limited gratefully acknowledges
the financial support of the Department of Canadian Heritage,
the Nova Scotia Department of Tourism and Culture
and the Canada Council for the Arts for our publishing program.

National Library of Canada Cataloguing in Publication

Sheldrick, Byron M.
Perils and possibilities : social activism and the law /
by Byron Sheldrick.

ISBN 1-55266-126-1

1. Social reformers—Legal status, laws, etc. 2. Political activists—Legal status,
laws, etc. 3. Dissenters—Legal status, laws, etc. I. Title.

K370.S46 2004   322.4   C2003-906849-8

Contents

To Robin, Lachlan and Morag

Acknowledgments

I lived with the idea for this book for a long time before it finally made its way to being written and, ultimately, published. Consequently, there are a number of people who require thanks.

First, my colleagues in the Department of Law at Keele University were enormously supportive and of invaluable assistance to me. Keele provided a stimulating intellectual environment for socio-legal studies and I have many fond memories of my time there. Special thanks to Didi Herman and Carl Stychin (now at the University of Reading) for taking a fellow Canuck under their wings and to Kenneth Armstrong (Queen Mary and Westfield College), Sally Sheldon, Doris Buss and Michael Thompson for their friendship and support. Second, my colleagues at the University of Winnipeg deserve special thanks for their role in the development of this project. Thanks to Jim Silver, whose need for coffee is almost as great as my own. Our conversations played an important role in the development of many of the ideas in this book. His engagement, as both an activist and an academic, is an example to anyone who believes that academics are removed from the real worlds of politics. Thanks also to Peter Ives, Joan Grace and Joanne Boucher—exceptional colleagues who have always been willing to both listen to and challenge my ideas. The University of Winnipeg provided me with a research leave in the spring of 2003. This was a valuable time, during which I wrote much of the manuscript. I also need to thank Wayne Antony at Fernwood Publishing, and Colin Mooers and Trevor Harrison. Their comments were extremely helpful in honing the arguments contained in the book and greatly improved the final product. Wayne also deserves thanks for being extremely patient when I missed deadlines. Thanks also to Jane Butler for her excellent editing, to Debbie Mathers for typing the final manuscript, to Brenda Conroy for proofreading and to Beverley Rach for the cover design and book layout. I also need to thank Ian Greene and George Szablowski of York University. Their encouragement and comments on my earlier work helped shape this project. A special thanks to Leo Panitch of York University. Leo has been an intellectual mentor and a close friend to myself and my family. His encouragement and support throughout my academic career have been invaluable.

Chapter 2 is a substantially revised version of a paper entitled "Law, Representation and Political Activism: Community-based Practice and the Mobilization of Legal Resources," that was published by the *Canadian Journal of Law and Society* 10 (1995).

I must also thank my family. My partner, Robin Alsop, has been endlessly supportive and tolerant of my late nights in front of the computer and my crankiness when the project was not going well. I cannot imagine having accomplished this without her in my life. My children, Lachlan and Morag, have also been tolerant (or at least as tolerant as one can expect of a six- and a three-year old) of Daddy's work. I'm sure Lachlan will recall the summer of 2003 as the one where his style was significantly cramped by my writing.

Finally, I need to thank the countless activists out there committed to social justice. This book is inspired by them.

Byron Sheldrick
November 2003, Winnipeg

Chapter 1

Introduction

Law, with its language of justice, fairness and equity, seems well suited to advancing claims for social justice. It is not surprising, therefore, that social movements frequently employ strategies and tactics centred around the concept of rights. This was as true of workers' movements in nineteenth-century England as it is of the gay and lesbian movement of today. At the same time, law seems to be a somewhat dangerous ally for social movements seeking to promote social transformation. The institutions of law are fundamentally conservative, slow to change and frequently operate to preserve and protect the rights and privileges of the powerful. In this sense, law operates as a force for social control, not for social change.[1] At that same time, those who hold power cannot completely ignore law's claims to fairness and equality without undermining the legitimacy of their own positions of influence and privilege.[2] In other words, the operation of law in society is highly contradictory. Law can be both empowering and constraining for social action groups promoting social and political change. The objective of this book is to explore this contradiction and to assist movements and movement activists in navigating the difficult terrain that is the legal landscape.[3]

In 1974 Marc Galanter wrote "Why the Haves Come Out Ahead," examining why we expect those with power and resources to do better before the courts than those without.[4] Litigants fall into two basic categories. "Repeat players," such as corporations, governments, prosecutors, and other large organizations, tend to be well-resourced and appear before the courts on a fairly regular basis. Repeat players can utilize resources to achieve beneficial results over the long term, even at the cost of sacrificing outcomes in specific individual cases. They also, because of their continued engagement with law, develop close ties and professional relationships with their lawyers. "One-shotters," by contrast, have fewer resources and appear before the court less frequently. One-shot litigants tend to have more at stake in any individual case, and because of the infrequency of their litigation, cannot build up the expertise and know-how to play for long-term benefits. Typical one-shotters include individuals, the criminally accused, persons contesting the terms of divorce, and so on. The horizon of the one-shot litigant is fixed firmly on the outcome of a particular case.

Although Galanter was not specifically concerned with the question of political activism his analysis is helpful. First, he quite rightly points to the importance of resources. Most social action groups will appear before the courts infrequently. Indeed, most social movements lack the financial resources to situate courts and law at the heart of their political strategy. Going to court is expensive. However, when social action groups do find themselves in court, they invariably confront opposing parties who, within Galanter's framework, constitute repeat players. Most notably, social action groups encounter corporate interests or the state when they venture into the legal realm. Examples come readily to mind: an environmental group seeking to halt a development project, a student group challenging restrictions on its right to demonstrate on campus, an anti-poverty or welfare rights group challenging cuts to social services. Even when social action groups do constitute repeat players before the courts, as sometimes happens, there may still be considerable resource differences between the groups and their opponents.

While Galanter felt that it was unlikely that the courts could be used to advance significant social change, he did argue that the "have nots" of the legal world might be able to organize themselves and develop resources to increase their effectiveness. One option is to develop legal expertise within the movement This route has been followed in the United States, with the development of specialized public interest law centres. The National Association for the Advancement of Colored People (NAACP), for example, has developed a coterie of legal experts in their fight to end discrimination against African-Americans. In Canada, the Women's Legal Education and Action Fund has pursued a similar strategy.[5] The result of this approach, however, is a tendency to favour law and legal strategies for achieving social change over and above other forms of political activism.

Galanter's work has led to an emphasis on the courts as the locus for the expression and articulation of law. Galanter was primarily concerned with explaining why groups with resources could generally be expected to fare better before the courts. This focus on courts has dominated many of the discussions of the utility and desirability of social action groups using the law as part of their political strategy. Gerald Rosenberg, in *The Hollow Hope,* even defines social change in terms of policy changes of a national scope that result directly from a judicial decision.[6] With such a narrow focus, it is hardly surprising that Rosenberg concludes that going to court will rarely produce social change. While it is true that courts and law will likely not produce social change, it is important to explore the extent to which they can be utilized to secure or advance claims of equality and justice. This is a much broader consideration and one that doesn't necessarily require us to focus on courts and their decisions as the sole instruments of political change.

The emphasis on courts is an enduring legacy of Galanter's work and has dominated the field of study. In both the United States and Canada, this is reflected in a concern with the successes and failures of public interest litigation. The measure of activism's success is the number of victories in the courts and whether those victories have "made a difference."[7] Perceptions about law and activism have been dominated by an approach that starts and ends with courts, and in particular, with the decisions of courts. Social movements are simply parties before the courts, rather than the central focus. Consequently, there has been little attempt to question the law from the perspective of the social action group.

Rather than beginning with judicial outcomes, we should set our sights on the tactical and strategic questions that law raises for social movements. Such an approach encourages us to consider the broader objectives of social movements but also to view law in a more varied and pluralistic fashion. Law is articulated not only by the courts, but by legislatures, prisons, welfare bureaucracies, administrative boards and tribunals and a host of other state structures.

Moreover, confronting law is not always a matter of choice for social action groups. We live in a world that is dominated by law and legal structures, and it may be that any strategy of political change will have to confront the law. A protest, which is far removed from a deliberate strategy of "going to court," will nevertheless involve engagements with legal structures. A permit may be required for a demonstration or a march. The police may intervene and arrest protesters. In 1997, demonstrations at the University of British Columbia against a meeting of the Asia–Pacific Economic Cooperation (APEC) resulted in a formal administrative hearing into police misconduct and brutality. Undoubtedly the activists who organized the anti-APEC demonstrations had no idea that their political point would be made through the Royal Canadian Mounted Police (RCMP) Public Complaints Commission. Nevertheless, this became the vehicle by which the activists could keep pressure on the government and raise awareness of their cause. In other instances, government or corporate interests may utilize the courts to deter activists by seeking either an injunction to prohibit their activities or damage awards that might financially cripple the group. The cost of defending the litigation may achieve this objective, regardless of the outcome of the specific case. These techniques have been used to prevent demonstrators from blockading logging roads or to financially attack those who organize consumer boycotts of a corporation's product. In all of these instances, the choice of engaging with law is not the social action group's to make but rather is forced upon them.

The tendency to focus on the courts when discussing the relationship between law and activism has been reflected in the Canadian debate around the *Canadian Charter of Rights and Freedoms*. This debate has focused on the implications of "going to court" for both social movements and for the broader political system. For those who are critical of the courts—"rights debunkers" as Didi Herman has termed them[8]—the primary concern is the anti-democratic and non-participatory implications of going to court. For those on the left of the political spectrum, law is understood as a demobilizing force that operates to limit the radicalism and participatory nature of social movement politics. Social movements, if they engage in legal activism, will lose control of their agenda to lawyers and judges who will transform their political issues into a narrow set of legal issues, thereby distorting and nullifying the transformative potential of the movement[9] The strategy of utilizing law and courts is disparagingly referred to as a form of "legalized" or "judicialized" politics. Courts, it is argued, should be shunned in favour of more democratic and participatory avenues of political activism. Unfortunately, the nature of these more "genuine" forms of political expression are rarely spelled out.

There are also critics of judicialized politics on the right of the political spectrum. Here the concern is not so much with the legalization of social movement politics but with the politicization of law by social movements. Morton and Knopff, for example, have argued that a "court party" of women's groups, gay and lesbian groups, Aboriginal people and other equity-seeking groups have used the courts to make political gains that could not be achieved through legislatures.[10] This, they argue, is un-democratic and represents a dangerous erosion of our parliamentary traditions. It shifts power away from elected officials and political parties to an unelected and unaccountable judiciary. For Morton and Knopff, social movements have used the courts to do an "end run" around the institutions of Canadian democracy. Ironically, Morton and Knopff do not see the primary role of courts as a constraint on social movements, but rather see judges as radicals and activists facilitating social movement agendas.

There is some truth in both the left and the right critiques of judicialized politics. Social movements do make use of the courts and do achieve important victories in that forum. Those victories often involve changes that are forced on reluctant and frequently hostile legislatures. Antonio Lamer, former chief justice of the Supreme Court of Canada, responded to criticisms that the court had become too activist by arguing that if Parliament acted to remedy injustices and inequalities, the court would not be forced to do so.[11] At the same time, it is also undoubtedly true that the reliance on courts may do little to foster real social change and may in fact blunt the edge of social movement activism. It has been forcefully argued, for example, that an over-reliance on judicial politics by the American women's movement has left it ill-equipped to fight against the state-led erosion of abortion rights. Similarly, three decades of civil rights litigation has, arguably, not substantially improved the conditions of the majority of African-Americans in the United States.[12]

Both these approaches conceptualize the relationship between law and activism from the perspective of the courts. They assume that activism around law and rights will take place in courts. They also assume both an idealized legislature and an idealized court, in that parliaments and legislatures are understood to be inherently democratic and participatory while courts are seen as inherently undemocratic and non-participatory. Legislatures, therefore, are the appropriate location for politics, while courts are the appropriate location for the practice of an idealized and non-political form of law. The broader structures of the state, and most particularly the undemocratic influence of the bureaucracy, is rarely considered in this framework.[13]

These approaches conceptualize politics and law in an "either/or" fashion: social action groups either engage in a genuine and democratic form of politics or they engage in an illegitimate and depoliticized form of judicialized politics. This position, ironically from both the left and the right critiques, however, is rarely based on solid empirical study of social movement practice. Rarely do social movements make this sort of stark choice. Rather, they employ a diversity of tactics and strategies, depending on the structure of political opportunities and the nature of the constraints and obstacles that they face at any particular moment[14] Approaches that focus on courtroom procedures fail to capture the dynamic nature of social movement practice, and consequently employ an understanding of law and activism that is far too static and limited.

In this book I approach the question of law and political activism from the point of view of the social movement. Tarrow has defined social movements as collective challenges, based on common purposes and social solidarities, to the power of elites and state authorities.[15] Legal structures and institutions can be one vehicle by which these challenges are expressed. However, social movements are also frequently characterized by a wide variety of social networks and may take a large number of organizational forms. For the purposes of this book, therefore, I will concentrate on social movement organizations rather than social movements in the broadest sense of the term. My concern is with the social action group that might confront law in the midst of a broader political campaign.

In considering law from the perspective of the social action group, it is necessary to take up Galanter's first premise—namely that the key to successfully engaging with law depends on the nature of the resources a group has available. Galanter's "repeat players" will likely always have an edge in terms of resource capacity. However, this does not mean social action groups lack the resources to incorporate law into their political strategies without the legal process overwhelming them.

One difficulty that any social action group faces when engaging with law is lack of expertise. As Carol Smart has argued, the power of law rests in its unique language and structure of thought, which permits it to "speak the truth" in a fashion that is difficult to challenge.[16] The law has the capacity to transform contentious political positions into rules supported by the legal system. While all of us have a sense of what the law is about, largely gleaned from the mass media, very few of us have the technical expertise to develop sophisticated legal arguments or represent ourselves in court. This is the near-exclusive preserve of the lawyer and the judge, carefully guarded by professional associations and the exclusive admission policies of law schools, which contribute to the mystique of law.[17]

The implications of pursuing a strategy of legal activism are therefore difficult to assess for social action groups. I once asked a group of third-year politics students in a human rights course to imagine a case in which university officials had discriminated against a group of students by banning them from forming an activist group on campus. I asked what steps they might take to try to force the administration to reverse its decision. Immediately the students came up with a number of ideas: a petition, a protest demonstration, the lobbying of faculty and university administrators, a sit-in. In the language of social movements, these are part of the "repertoire" of political action with which we are familiar. Even those who are not politically active can imagine these possibilities and begin mobilizing to realize them. I then asked the students what they would do if all of these tactics failed. After much prompting, someone suggested litigation and a human rights challenge. Despite their rights-based discourse on the issues on which their political campaign would be built, litigation was the students' choice of last resort. What would be the first step in pursuing a legal challenge, I asked? How would they go about it? The only suggestion was to hire a lawyer, although the students did not have a good idea of the process involved. Beyond simply contacting a lawyer, the world of judicialized politics was a mystery to them. This was a repertoire of political action with which the students were unfamiliar.

This example highlights several important points. First, most people will not immediately consider pursuing a court challenge. Most of us know that this is expensive, time consuming and the costs of failure potentially steep. Social action groups understand that litigation will take valuable resources away from their other activities and so, in most instances, it is a step taken only reluctantly and as a last resort. Social action groups will tend to prefer repertoires of political action with which they are familiar. New tactics of political activism will develop of course, but the group is unlikely to adopt a strategy for which its members lack expertise and capacity.

Second, the example points to the centrality of lawyers and legal expertise. One cannot contemplate complex political action on legal issues without engaging with the legal profession. This raises important issues about the structure of the legal profession and the nature of legal representation. It may be difficult to hold lawyers accountable to movement goals and objectives. Much will depend on the individual lawyer, but also on the nature of the group and what it hopes to achieve, as well as the type of case and the nature of the legal issues (which may not always be the same as the political issues) it raises.

Third, concepts of rights and justice are important "frames" through which social movements articulate their political program to a broader audience. These are shared understandings that allow us to articulate grievances and injustices in terms that mobilize political action. My students recognized this when they chose to discuss the university's actions in terms of rights, even though they were not contemplating litigation. Use of this discourse does not necessarily involve going to court. At the same time, taking an action to court may give the group a profile and a media presence that might otherwise be difficult to achieve. The legal action may provide a unique and important opportunity to develop a case that goes beyond the court to the broader public.

This book, then, explores the contradictory nature of law and political activism and attempts to shed some light on the tactical and strategic questions that social action groups face upon engaging with law. In this regard, I hope to go beyond "either/or" tendencies and develop a better understanding of social action group goals and objectives when confronting law. This should permit a better appreciation of both the opportunities and constraints presented by a strategy of legal activism.

At the same time, this book is also intended as a resource for activists and social action groups engaged with law. I certainly don't seek to turn activists into lawyers, but rather to provide them with sufficient information to weigh the pros and cons of going to court and understand how law intersects with other dimensions of their political struggles. In a sense, this book is to help break down the lawyer's monopoly on expertise and assist social action groups in their dealings with the legal profession.

To that end, Chapter 2 elaborates on the themes developed above and examines theoretical perspectives on law and political activism. In particular, it expands on the notion that law is both a potential resource for social movements and also a potential constraint. Central to this thesis is the belief that the power of law, as a means of social control and as a depoliticizing force, rests in the exclusivity of legal expertise. I examine the nature of legal reasoning and the conceptions of legal representation to shed light on how lawyers control clients and limit the potential of utilizing law as a tool of political change. The development of alternative sources of legal expertise, such as community-based legal clinics or "people's law schools," as well as the restructuring of legal professionalism, are considered as vehicles for breaking down the law's monopoly on expertise.

Chapter 3 begins an examination of law intersecting with social movement politics through the control and regulation of protest and dissent. To a certain extent this chapter is intended to demonstrate that social movements cannot escape law, in that legal regulation is one of the state's main vehicles for controlling dissent. I examine the implications of criminal law powers on protest, the capacity of police forces to regulate and disrupt protests, the implications of recent anti-terrorist measures and the capacity of municipalities to regulate demonstrations, parades, strikes and other types of protest gatherings. It is also true, however, that the state is not the only power that can invoke the law to control dissent This chapter also examines how corporations use courts and law in a pre-emptive manner against activists through SLAPPs (strategic litigation against public participation). The chapter concludes by considering the civil liberties implications raised by these questions.

Chapter 4 continues where Chapter 3 leaves off, providing a more comprehensive examination of civil liberties and human rights issues. Rights provide a powerful discourse that is frequently utilized by social movements to frame issues, mobilize members and communicate to the broader public. This chapter examines how the protection of rights in formal constitutional documents, such as the *Canadian Charter of Rights and Freedoms* or the American *Bill of Rights*, provides an important resource for social action groups, but also a potential limit on their activities. This chapter examines how certain types of rights claims may be more valuable to social action groups than others.

Chapter 5 examines the difficult decisions involved in going to court, provides an overview of the court system structure and considers the tactical and strategic questions activists might wish to address before going to court. This includes what to expect when dealing with a lawyer, how to choose a lawyer, and the costs of judicial action. This chapter also includes several case studies of social action groups going before the courts to highlight these issues.

Chapter 6 continues by examining the significance of the administrative state. Courts are only one forum in which "judicial" decision-making takes place. Labour boards, welfare appeal boards, workers compensation tribunals, environmental assessment boards and other similar state regulatory agencies may be appropriate legal venues for activists. This chapter discusses these institutions, how they operate, the advantages and disadvantages of appearing before them and the opportunities for appealing administrative decisions to the courts.

The examples in this book are primarily Canadian, although I also refer to movements and cases from elsewhere, particularly the United States and Britain. I do this in part because I am most familiar with Canada. I also do it because the tactical choices for any social action group confronting the law depend very much on the particular legal system with which they must deal. Rules of standing, the powers of administrative tribunals, police powers to arrest demonstrators and the scope of constitutional rights will all vary from country to country. This book would have been written very differently prior to Canada's adoption of the *Canadian Charter of Rights and Freedoms* (or more likely would not have been written at all). To do justice to the myriad of differences between complex legal systems would have defeated one of the primary objectives of the book, namely to provide an accessible and useful resource to activists and students. The broad themes discussed in the book, however, are applicable and relevant to almost any jurisdiction.

The book is also a guide to on-line legal resources. Appendix 1 includes links to the texts of important rights documents, including the *Canadian Charter of Rights and Freedoms*, the American *Bill of Rights* and the *European Convention on Human Rights*. It also provides an extensive list of legal resources that might prove useful to activists and those who lack formal legal training. Included are links to public legal information centres, community legal clinics and other sources of advice and assistance. Many of these sources share a political commitment to social justice. Social action groups need access to these organizations and their expertise if they are to bring law into the movement without allowing it to colonize their objectives and aspirations.

Notes

1. For an interesting discussion of the relationship between law and order, see Wade Mansell, Belinda Meteyard and Alan Thomson, *A Critical Introduction to Law* (London: Cavendish Publishing Ltd., 1995), ch. 2.
2. C.B. MacPherson, *The Life and Times of Liberal Democracy* (Oxford: Oxford University Press, 1977) discusses how the expansion of democratic political rights flowed from the contradictory logic of equality embedded in liberal economic thought.
3. The contradiction at the heart of the law/activism question has been the subject of much inquiry. Some have argued that law offers, at best, only a limited potential for advancing progressive political objectives. Victories in court, it is argued, will frequently prove to be pyrrhic in nature: won at too great a cost to the victor. See Judy Fudge and Harry Glasbeek, "The Politics of Rights: A Politics with Little Class," *Social and Legal Studies* 1 (1992), p. 45–70. Others, while not unaware of the limits of law, have accepted more readily the importance and utility of law for political activism. See, for example, Michael McCann, "Legal Mobilization and Social Reform Movements: Notes on Theory and Its Applications," *Studies in Law, Politics and Society* 11 (1991), p. 225–54; Didi Herman, "Beyond the Rights Debate," *Social and Legal Studies* 2 (1993), p. 25–43; Miriam Smith, *Lesbian and Gay Rights in Canada: Social Movements and Equality Seeking 1971–1995* (Toronto: University of Toronto Press, 1999).
4. Marc Galanter, "Why the Haves Come out Ahead, Speculations on the Limits of Social Change," *Law and Society Review* 9 (1974), p. 95–160. Galanter's work has been the subject of much commentary, including a symposium that appeared in the *Law and Society Review* 33 (1999) to mark the 25th anniversary of its publication. Some of the papers in that symposium include: Patricia Ewick and Susan Silbey, "Common Knowledge and Ideological Critique: The Significance of Knowing that the 'Haves' Come Out Ahead"; Richard Lempert, "A Classic at 25: Reflections on Galanter's 'Haves' Article and Work It Has Inspired"; Joel Grossman, Herbert Kritzer

and Stewart Macaulay, "Do the 'Haves' Still Come Out Ahead?"; Charles Epp, "The Two Motifs of 'Why the 'Haves' Come out Ahead' and its Heirs."

5. Sherene Razack, *Canadian Feminism and the Law; The Women's Legal Education and Action Fund and the Pursuit of Equality* (Toronto: Second Story Press, 1991).

6. Gerald Rosenberg, *The Hollow Hope: Can Courts Bring about Social Change?* (Chicago: University of Chicago Press, 1991).

7. Judy Fudge and Harry Glasbeek, "The Politics of Rights," supra. note 3. For a criticism of this approach see Didi Herman, "Beyond the Rights Debate," supra. note 3.

8. Didi Herman, "The Good, the Bad, and the Smugly: Sexual Orientation and Perspectives on the Charter," in David Schneiderman and Kate Sutherland (eds.), *Charting the Consequences: The Impact of Charter Rights on Canadian Law and Politics* (Toronto: University of Toronto Press, 1997).

9. See, for example, Michael Mandel, *The Charter of Rights and the Legalization of Politics in Canada* (Toronto: Thompson, 1994); Allen Hutchinson and Andrew Petter, "Private Rights/Public Wrongs: The Liberal Lie of the Charter," *University of Toronto Law Journal* 38 (1988), p. 178.

10. F.L. Morton and Rainer Knopff, *The Charter Revolution and the Court Party* (Peterborough: Broadview Press, 2000). For an excellent critique of the position, see Wayne McKay, "The Legislature, the Executive and the Courts: The Delicate Balance of Power or Who is Running This Country Anyway?" *Dalhousie Law Journal* 24(2) (2001), p. 39–74.

11. Kirk Makin, "We are not Gunslingers," *Globe and Mail*, Tues. April 9, 2002, p. A4. Reg Whitaker has also argued that judicial review by courts is valuable because the intensely political nature of certain issues makes elected officials unwilling to deal with them. See Reg Whitaker, "Rights in a Free and Democratic Society: Abortion," in David Shugarman and Reg Whitaker (eds.), *Federalism and Political Community* (Peterborough: Broadview Press, 1989).

12. See, for example, Alan Freeman, "Anti-discrimination Law: The View from 1989," in David Kairys, *The Politics of Law: A Progressive Critique* (New York: Pantheon Books, 1990).

13. I have made this point elsewhere. See B. Sheldrick, "Law, Representation and Political Activism: Community-based Practice and the Mobilization of Legal Resources," *Canadian Journal of Law and Society Community Legal Practice* 10 (1995), p. 155–84.

14. See Sydney Tarrow, *Power in Movement: Social Movements and Contentious Politics* (2nd ed). (Cambridge: Cambridge University Press, 1998), ch. 5.

15. Ibid, p. 2.

16. Carol Smart, *Feminism and the Power of Law* (London: Routledge, 1989).

17. Jamie Cassels and Maureen Maloney, "Critical Legal Education: Paralysis with a Purpose," *Canadian Journal of Law and Society* 4 (1990), p. 99.

Chapter 2

Social Movements and Law
Perils, Pitfalls and Possibilities

Rights and Law: Contradictions in Legal Structures

Most critics of social movements engaging with law focus on the ideological underpinnings of law and the undemocratic nature of judicial processes. Fudge and Glasbeek, for example, argued that adopting law as part of a political strategy necessarily involves acceptance of the basic principles of liberalism, which underpin legal institutions and legal thinking.[1] Those principles, which emphasize individual rights over collective interests and centrality of private property and capitalist market economics, are seen as antithetical to the development of radical political alternatives. At the same time, the undemocratic nature of the judicial process means there is little that social movements can do to alter or shift the ideological underpinnings of the courts. Once in the judicial arena, the movement risks losing control of its agenda to lawyers and judges who monopolize the process. While there may be lawyers and judges committed to principles of social justice, the overall structure of the courts is conservative and devoted to maintenance of the status quo.

There is much in this vision of law that must be taken seriously. It provides a powerful corrective to conventional wisdom and its emphasis on the neutrality of law and the importance of formal legal equality. Nevertheless, there are several difficulties with this argument. It assumes that political activism involving law takes place only in the courts and therefore doesn't consider the impact of law on social movement politics in the context of the movement's broader political agenda and political activism. Consequently, it provides an extremely deterministic understanding of the relationship between social movements and law, in which law's influence is virtually unlimited and automatic.[2] Fudge and Glasbeek argue that there is little or no opportunity to engage in struggles around the definitions of rights and to utilize those struggles as vehicles for political mobilization and movement building. Any such attempt will be "blocked" by utilizing the language and tools of socially dominant groups.[3] Similarly, Hutchinson and Petter have argued that attempting to use courts as vehicles of political change means abandoning any project of radical social transformation. The ideological underpinnings of law accept the existence of private property and the power that goes along with it, while characterizing the state as a potential threat to individual liberty and freedom. They argue that this constitutes a form of "legal liberalism" that leads us to abandon the state as a potential ally in the quest for social justice and to ignore the dangers of concentrations of private power that constitute the real obstacle to social justice.[4]

The actual practices of social movements, however, lead us to question these conclusions. Even if social movements must engage with the language and discourse of legal liberalism when approaching the courts, this does not necessarily mean they will adopt the ideological perspective of the court into their core values and perspectives. Critics mistakenly assume that social movements seek to achieve radical social transformation through the courts, as opposed to utilizing the courts as part of a broader campaign of social transformation.

This approach to rights and law denies the potential for subverting what appears to be a monolithic and oppressive legal structure. Certainly it is true that law is one of the primary mechanisms of social control within capitalist society. It is also true that law legitimates private property and individualized social relations. Nevertheless, the law is often contradictory and flexible in its application, particularly to social circumstances. It is precisely for this reason that virtually all social movements of the past century, including workers' movements, have relied on a discourse of rights.[5] The logic of equality that informs this rights discourse and law's own vision of itself is malleable and potentially politically empowering. Employing such a discourse does not automatically lead to accepting the dominant definition of those rights, nor does it automatically mean abandoning radicalism. Rather, the ability to transcend dominant views of the world is a question of political organization and mobilization

This is well demonstrated by the abortion rights movement in Canada. The Canadian Abortion Rights Action League made a deliberate strategic decision to pursue a court case as the vehicle to attack the criminalization of abortion in Canada.[6] Although the movement was ultimately successful in having the criminal provisions that made abortion illegal struck down by the Supreme Court of Canada, there were many losses in lower courts along the way. The failure at any particular level of court, however, was simply one setback within a broader political struggle. In this sense, it differed little from a lobby strategy that fails to yield substantive changes to state policy. Those involved in the abortion rights movement did not simply accept judicial pronouncements that denied the inclusion of reproductive freedom and choice as part of women's human rights. Rather, they held demonstrations to coincide with the release of judicial decisions. These could either be a celebration of a victory or a condemnation of "sexist judges" in the case of defeat. In the latter case, the narrow reading of rights by the court was translated by the social movement into its own discourse and became the subject of ridicule and scorn. Rallies and demonstrations became opportunities to demystify the court and to situate it within the broader context of a state that was hostile to women's interests and to the expansion of abortion rights.

It rarely happens that social movement organizations pursuing radical change find a forum for their activism that is not, in some respects, hostile. Rights critics emphasize the unique nature of legal reasoning and its capacity to claim neutrality and objectivity. The political nature of issues, they argue, is obscured within a discourse dominated by questions of legality; political activism is replaced with a reliance on legal technique as a mechanism for solving problems.[7] The uniqueness of law's claim to neutrality stems largely from the continued separation of the legal and political spheres—the judicial and the legislative branches of government—and the failure to consider courts within the broader context of the state.

Contradictions in the Bureaucratic State

Within the context of the modern bureaucratic state, however, courts are not alone in employing a discourse rooted in claims to (scientific) objectivity and neutrality in order to depoliticize issues. Bureaucratic agencies, for example, rely on the distinction between politics and administration to legitimate their role in the policy process. Administration, like law, seeks to translate political issues into problems of technique, thereby depoliticizing and demobilizing opposition groups and structuring the nature of participation within the state.[8] Despite this, however, many groups avoid the dangers of co-optation and attempt to exploit the contradictions of the state. Any social movement seeking to influence state policy must confront ideological practices that are antagonistic to its own. The degree to which these antagonistic ideologies can be transcended (or escaped) depends, at least to some extent, on the group's own organizational structure and ideological practices. Thus, groups need to be strategic in their approaches to state institutions. Indeed, there is a significant body of literature, both within the social movement and academic communities, that attempts to demystify administrative practices and provide the strategic resources needed to avoid co-optation on the terrain of the state.[9]

The contradictions of the administrative state are often exploited in debates over the meaning and shape of welfare state capitalism. Claus Offe, for example, has outlined how the state, driven by its own need for legitimacy and the desire to safeguard the conditions of its rule, must reconcile pressures to reproduce a market society that enhances capital accumulation with the creation of socially necessary activities and policies, including social welfare policies, that exist outside the market. This has resulted in opportunities for struggle that further exacerbate those contradictions and make those activities and policies, such as health care and education, important sites for political struggle.[10]

The state must balance its need to foster and encourage capitalism with its need to protect vulnerable groups and individuals from the effects of capitalism. It attempts to legitimate these efforts using a discourse of administrative neutrality and objectivity. The growing importance of law and legal regulation can be understood within the context of these contradictions. As they become increasingly difficult to manage, the discourse of administrative neutrality can no longer be maintained. Recourse to quasi-judicial administrative bodies and complex regulations around eligibility and reporting requirements serve to police and supervise welfare state programs while utilizing law's capacity to claim neutrality and objectivity.

Thus, law comes to be integrated into the material structure of the state in an increasingly complex fashion. That is, "[the] specificity of law and the juridical system [becomes] inscribed in the peculiar institutional structure of the capitalist State."[11] For Poulantzas, law played an important role in supporting the "centralizing-bureaucratic-hierarchic framework" of the state. This facilitated increased specialization in the nature of legal institutions and the development of a corps of "specialized jurists." As law becomes both an increasingly important mode of regulation and a characterizing element of state structure, state personnel become privileged in their ability to "know the law." This monopoly of knowledge plays an important role in "damp[ing] down and channel[ling] political crises, in such a way that they do not lead to crises of the State itself."[12]

Some legal scholars, such as Sally Merry and Boaventura de Souza Santos, have attempted to develop a more complex and sophisticated understanding of the pluralistic and fragmented nature of law within advanced capitalist societies.[13] They are critical of the tendency to ignore the state and assume a "unitary legal system based on universal and abstract laws applied by an independent judiciary."[14] By focusing attention away from the official institutional sites of legal discourse, such as courts, these observers have identified a plurality of legal orders existing within the same political structures. The state itself becomes a problematic social actor in its ordering of social relations through policy fields, which generates distinct legal realms. Santos has called the resulting complex patterns "micro-states." This approach begins the task of integrating our conception of law with an understanding of the state as fragmented and contradictory, expanding our understanding of the concept of law and its relationship to the political. As Santos has said, "[t]he analytical focus must … be on the state as contested terrain, a social field in which state and non-state, local and transnational social relations interact, merge and conflict in dynamic and even volatile combinations."[15] This requires a consideration of how law and legal relations manifest themselves in a variety of institutional and social contexts, as well as the possibilities for political action and conventional liberal assumptions regarding the nature of law and politics.

The traditional debate about rights and political activism, which restricts its consideration of law to its interpretation in the courts, fails to address the complexities of law and its relationship to the operation of the welfare state as a whole. The economically and politically dispossessed, for example, often experience law within the context of the state so that sharp distinctions between law and politics, or courts and legislatures, have little meaning to them. Legal codes, as articulated and enforced by the welfare official, the unemployment insurance system, or workers' compensation doctors, are far more relevant to the lives of many people than the debates about courts versus legislatures. Moreover, it is on this terrain that anti-poverty activists and workers' rights advocates most often encounter law.

Legal Mobilization Strategies

Recently, attempts have been made to explore more concretely the potential and limits of struggle around conceptions of rights and law.[16] From this perspective, law, like other institutions of liberal-democracy, provides both political opportunities and political dangers for social movements. Law and rights are seen as both providing strategic resources for popular mobilization and constraining social action groups. The primary emphasis is on integrating law into a broader political strategy and going beyond its restrictive articulation in official institutional sites.[17] Legal resources become important elements of the political campaigns that include a multiplicity of state and non-state institutions and structures.

Like the legal pluralists, this approach considers the hegemonic nature of law to be partial and incomplete. As Michael McCann has argued,

> system wide patterns of hegemony are always maintained by an incomplete and unstable process of diverse, site-specific accom-modations between domination and resistance. Hence, whereas law in the aggregate surely tends to support definable hegemonic patterns of power, we must be attentive to the variable, shifting dynamics of power-laden legal conventions and practices within different contexts.[18]

Consequently, while law may support the status quo and operate as a means of social control, that control is incomplete and can be contested. Law is multi-faceted and pluralistic in nature, rather than closed and monolithic. The open and malleable nature of rights, then, becomes a distinct advantage in that political action around rights claims can become an important vehicle for articulating social conflicts and contradictions. The possibility arises for the creative use of law within broader political struggles.

This perspective is neither for nor against rights. Rather, it simply views rights and law as a potential resource in political struggles. Law is seen as an important terrain for engaging in struggle. Pro-rights advocates, therefore, are not advocating a headlong rush to embrace law and legal struggle as the answer to the failure of so-called "old-style" politics.[19] Rather, they call for a considered and strategic approach to questions of law and rights, one that exploits the contradictory and pluralistic nature of law within advanced industrial societies.

In directing our attention away from the law-politics dichotomy, an opportunity arises to examine more closely how individuals interact with state legal institutions. Consequently, just as we should be cautious about integrating law into political struggles, we should also be sceptical and cautious about the broader state. The "legalization of politics," from this perspective, is not the by-product of entrenched bills of rights, but rather is part and parcel of the modern state. Consequently, the creation of new state agencies and programs also carries the potential for reproducing the depoliticizing aspects of both law and administration.[20] Social movements need to engage in many different arenas of struggle, both administrative and legal, state-centred and de-centred, recognizing the constraints and opportunities presented by each.

In this sense, Michael McCann's work has been particularly important in that he attempts to delineate several different ways in which legal mobilization strategies can contribute to a political campaign. He argues that legal mobilization is most useful for its indirect consequences rather than for directly winning gains through litigation.[21] In particular, McCann sees legal mobilization as playing an important role in movement building, in negotiating reform policies with state actors and in implementing reforms. Finally, legal reform action leaves an important legacy for subsequent movement development and struggle by laying a groundwork of expectations and aspirations among group members.

This perspective allows us to go beyond an analysis of the obvious institutional differences between courts and legislatures. It broadens our focus from law as it is articulated in courts to a consideration of state law in terms of legislation, regulation and administrative discretion. It questions how social action groups interrelate with these state structures that exert social control in a variety of "juridified" forms and contexts.

While it is important and salutory to consider the strategic possibilities of legal mobilization, rights advocates must nonetheless answer some of the most important and pressing challenges posed by their critics. In particular, there is the organizational difficulty of integrating a strategic understanding of law into a social movement's overall agenda. Given the general acceptance that litigation in and of itself will not lead to profound social change, there is a pressing need to confront the limits of and obstacles to a legal mobilization strategy.

All political strategies raise a number of tactical questions. Problems associated with gaining access to the state, deploying scarce resources and balancing the need to mobilize a broad constituency with the need to lobby and consult with government officials; all need to be addressed. In the legal context similar issues must be dealt with. Questions of access arise when deciding between initiating an action as a party or intervening in the disputes of others. If the decision is made to intervene, should it be early in the trial process, thereby ensuring the maximum scope for participation in the development of the evidence record, or should it be delayed until the appeal stage, thereby acquiring a more limited role, but also saving considerable resources? The answers to these questions, of course, must be balanced by an appreciation of what remedies can be hoped for from the court in the case of victory. Will the court even be able to make the sort of remedial order being sought? Assessing these issues is further complicated by trying to understand the various indirect consequences of a legal strategy.

The difficulty of a legal mobilization strategy is not that the questions it poses for a social movement are so different from the questions posed by any other political strategy. Legal mobilization strategies are problematic because the capacity to develop responses to those questions is cloaked in a professional knowledge and expertise which most social action groups and individuals do not possess. All political campaigns and strategies require some degree of expertise. However, the specialized knowledge and expertise demanded by most political strategies can often be acquired through experience. The collective memory of the group serves as an important resource for dealing with problems associated with lobbying, protests, demonstrations and coalition building. These have become common in our shared repertoires of political action.

A legal mobilization strategy, on the other hand, involves a delegation of activism to lawyers and other legal professionals. The direction and objectives of a political project, therefore, are influenced, and potentially distorted, by a dependence on the legal profession. This makes it difficult to integrate a legal campaign into the broader political agenda of a social movement.

Generally, while critics of legalized politics may overestimate the ideological dangers of going to court, advocates of legal activism have not adequately addressed the potential influence of lawyers and the nature of legal representation. Lawyers are often treated as neutral instruments, devoid of ideological orientations. In other instances, it is simply assumed that progressive and activist lawyers will be hired and that this will be sufficient to ensure "representation" that is consistent with the group's overall objectives.[22]

If social movements are to successfully navigate the legal terrain, then, it is necessary to develop sources of expertise and knowledge that permit activists to engage with lawyers and the legal profession. This does not mean transforming activists into lawyers, but it does mean equipping activists with the tools necessary to understand legal strategies and their implications for the group's political agenda.

Legal Representation and Accountability:
Separating the Professional from the Political

An analysis of legal education and concepts of legal professionalism leads to concern about the role of lawyers in social movement politics. The capacity of lawyers to adequately represent political movements needs to be viewed with some scepticism. Consequently, social action groups need to develop resources and organizational structures that overcome professional monopolies of expertise and knowledge and permit the integration of legal knowledge into their political campaigns.

Generally, legal education emphasizes values that maintain the status quo.[23] Law school pedagogy, for example, is often premised on a technical approach to legal analysis that divorces individual cases from their social and political contexts. More radical and critical courses are often viewed as electives and ancillary to the core curriculum. Consequently, even those lawyers committed to social activism and social change tend to define political activism in terms that are relatively conservative and do not threaten the general political and economic framework of liberal-democracy. Robert Granfield has demonstrated that even radical law students redefine their concepts of social justice and political involvement to be consistent with large-firm life and the occasional pro bono case, rather than the more radical and participatory forms of community involvement and social activism.[24]

These values are strengthened by a professional ideology that emphasizes autonomy and independence from clients. Independence and autonomy are essential components of the legal profession's capacity to control expertise as a commodity for sale and to dictate its market value.[25] Lawyers, by virtue of their monopoly on expertise, exercise considerable control over clients and have a virtually unlimited capacity to shape the direction of a particular case. The choice of arguments, how those arguments will be presented and so on are all largely within the exclusive purview of the lawyer. While in theory lawyers seek instructions from clients, in reality lack of understanding of legal issues leads clients to defer to the professionals. This may result in a strategy for winning a case when a victory may in fact mean the narrowing of possibilities for future political action and gains.

In many ways, the lawyers' representative function is a unique feature of legal professionalism.[26] The nature of that representation, however, is quite limited and narrow. Representation is subsumed under a market relationship within which technical expertise is bought and sold. The market mechanism creates the illusion that legal services are simply a commodity that is readily available to anybody. The lawyer-client relationship is reduced to a simple contractual arrangement, thereby minimizing consideration of the manner by which that relationship structures power and knowledge. This, in turn, contributes to a professional ethos that conceptualizes all clients as the same. Since lawyers are selling an objective set of skills and services that can be applied to any client, there is little need to understand those "non-legal" factors that make certain clients unique. This has also fostered a professional attitude that minimizes political commitment on the part of legal practitioners.

Accountability, under such an approach, is limited to a narrow range of competency issues and issues of professional misconduct. Accountability does not go beyond the narrow terms of the market transaction. The nature of this relationship ensures the independence of the lawyer from the broader political and social objectives of the client. Broader concepts of accountability and representation are precluded by the dominant professional ideology and its emphasis on a technical approach to legal issues and a limited concept of representation and accountability.

This narrow approach to representation, unfortunately, has often been adopted as the appropriate model for public interest law as well. Public interest lawyers often feel considerable hostility from the legal profession. Consequently, there is tremendous pressure to reassert one's "professionalism." This can mean adopting models of representation, borrowed from the private bar, that are inappropriate for the political context of a public interest practice.[27] We need, then, to begin developing new conceptions of representation and accountability that carry with them the potential for mobilizing and politicizing communities, rather than relegating them to the status of client.

The ideological separation of lawyers from the political and social struggles of their clients points to the need for social action groups to develop their own capacity to deal with legal issues. This does not mean that social activists need to become legal experts. It does mean, however, that activists and leaders of social movements need to be able to assess the merits and demerits of legal strategies and make decisions as to how those strategies may be combined with their broader political objectives.

It is in this regard that an understanding of the role of expertise in political mobilization is necessary. Law's claim to neutrality and objectivity is as much about the exclusivity of legal knowledge as it is about the law itself. Consequently, we must pay attention to how legal resources are organized. The professional organization of most legal services embodies concepts of representation that may not be particularly amenable to the integration of legal strategies into broader political agendas.

The capacity of lawyers to direct and control their clients rests on two underpinnings of the legal profession: the profession's claim to exclusive control over legal knowledge and expertise and a concept of legal professionalism that requires a lawyer's legal practice to be separate and distinct from the political aspirations of her clients. Both these elements can be challenged.

The profession's capacity to control legal knowledge and the provision of legal services has been eroded by the emergence of community-based legal clinics, the increasing numbers of paralegals performing tasks that were once reserved for lawyers and the growth of administrative tribunals and boards where representatives are not required to be lawyers. At the same time, many high schools and universities now offer courses in law oriented towards those who might not pursue a career in law. Political science, human rights, public administration, sociology and criminology are all disciplines that increasingly have a component of legal education. The Internet has also greatly expanded access to legal resources and research material, demystifying law in much the same way that it has demystified the medical profession. Whereas, in the past, something as simple as looking up legislation might have required a trip to a law library, the full text of most laws is now readily available online. At the same time, there is a growing movement calling for the writing of both statutes and judicial decisions in clearer and more accessible language.

The profession's ideological commitment to autonomy and control is also contested. Robert Nelson and David Trubek have argued that legal professionalism is not a fixed, unitary set of values but "consists of multiple visions of what constitutes proper behavior by lawyers."[28] This approach builds on the work of Pierre Bourdieu, who argues that the legal profession is deeply structured and exerts tremendous force on those who come within its ambit. This force is a product of the deep structures of behaviour, which Bourdieu terms "habitus," generated by tradition, education and the daily experience of legal custom and professional usage.[29]

For Bourdieu, however, the legal habitus is not uncontested. Rather, like other social fields, it is a site of struggle for control and dominance. The nature of the field defines what is to be controlled and locates the issues in dispute. The struggle for control over the legal profession as a whole leads to a hierarchical system within the field. Different levels of professional prestige and power are attached to specific legal specialities and approaches. This ordering results in a hegemonic balance that ensures the relative stability of the profession. The understanding of the profession and legal ideology as contested and hierarchically ordered contrasts sharply with traditional assumptions of all lawyers and all areas of legal practice as essentially the same.

This approach permits social movements to consider the development of alternative conceptions of legal practice and the possibility of seeking out legal practitioners who will be more open to associating themselves with social movement objectives. There are numerous examples of this sort of legal practice. Small law firms, for example, often specialize in labour law for trade unions, human rights law or social issues from an explicitly feminist perspective. At the same time, community legal clinics, accountable to community boards of directors and employing non-lawyers as community organizers, offer a potentially more politicized alternative to conventional law firms.[30] In the United States, public interest law centres seek to develop specialized litigation expertise and pursue test cases outside the mainstream of the legal profession. The development of "people's law schools," such as the one in Vancouver, and more radical approaches to legal education, such as that attempted at Northwestern University in New York, also raise the possibility of learning law in a fashion that is more open to a political understanding of legal practice.[31]

These types of experiments can be categorized as examples of "cause lawyering." The parameters of cause lawyering are very broad and include such diverse practices as human rights law, environmental law, poverty law, labour law, public interest litigation (although each of these may also be practised in a fashion that would not be understood as "cause lawyering"). This also includes orientations to legal practice that have been variously defined as "critical lawyering," "feminist lawyering" and "radical lawyering."[32] It is possible, however, to identify some common threads that link different forms of cause lawyering. Most important, cause lawyers view themselves as morally and politically committed to the causes they represent. This identification with the client transcends the traditional market-oriented view of the lawyer–client relationship. Cause lawyering frequently aims to challenge the social, economic and political order and to place the legal professional in the midst of the struggle. Most of the attention to cause lawyering, however, focuses on lawyers rather than on movements. Legal professionals, regardless of their commitment and dedication to a cause, possess a knowledge and expertise that puts them in a position of power over their clients. Either lawyers need to become part of the movement itself, so that their activities become subject to the group's broader decision-making processes, or groups themselves need to develop a greater capacity to understand and deal with legal issues. Or both. In either instance, the question is one of resources and resource mobilization. Legal expertise needs to become a resource within the movement, rather than an externally imposed constraint on the movement's activities.

The development of legal practices that support cause lawyering is an important step in this direction, but it is not sufficient in and of itself. This is because the cause lawyer, however well intentioned, often gets involved in the political struggle only at the point of litigation. Social movements need to understand how the law impacts on the range of their activities and how different tactics and strategies raise legal issues. This theme is taken up more concretely in the next chapter, which examines the legal regulation of protest and dissent.

Notes

1. Judy Fudge and Harry Glasbeek, "The Politics of Rights: A Politics with Little Class," *Social and Legal Studies* 1(1992), p. 45–70.
2. Didi Herman, "Beyond the Rights Debate," *Social and Legal Studies* 2 (1993), p. 25–43 at 32.
3. Fudge and Glasbeek, supra. note. 1, p. 58–59.
4. Allen Hutchinson and Andrew Petter, "Private Rights/Public Wrongs: The Liberal Lie of the Charter," *University of Toronto Law Journal* 38 (1988), p. 178.
5. For a classic historical discussion of the contradictory relationship between law and politics, see E.P. Thompson, *Whigs and Hunters: The Origins of the Black Act* (London: Allan Lane, 1975). See also Noel Thompson, *The People's Science: The Popular Political Economy of Exploitation and Crisis, 1816–1834* (Cambridge: Cambridge University Press, 1984) for a discussion of how early workers' campaigns for democratic rights were combined with a sophisticated critique of capitalism and a radical political agenda.
6. For a discussion of the politics of the pro-choice movement in Canada, see Patricia Antonyshyn, B. Lee and Alex Merrill, "Marching for Women's Lives: The Campaign for Free-Standing Abortion Clinics in Ontario," in Frank Cunningham et al. (eds.), *Social Movements/Social Change: The Politics and Practice of Organizing* (Toronto: Between the Lines, 1988). See also Shelly Gavigan, "Morgentaler and Beyond: Abortion, Reproduction and the Courts," in Janine Brodie, Shelly Gavigan and Jane Jenson, *The Politics of Abortion* (Toronto: Oxford University Press, 1992), p. 117, for a discussion of how the pro-choice movement's understanding of rights changed during the post-*Morgentaler* period. Gavigan also provides an account of how the anti-abortion movement continues to define abortion and arguments about foetal rights in terms that are not judicially endorsed.
7. See, for example, Michael Mandel, *The Charter of Rights and Freedoms and the Legalization of Politics in Canada* (Toronto: Thompson, 1994), p. 51–59. For a discussion of this from a more post-modern perspective, see Carol Smart, *Feminism and the Power of Law* (New York: Routledge, 1989).
8. See Nicos Poulantzas, *State, Power, Socialism* (London, New Left Books, 1978), p. 58–60. Poulantzas argued that official discourses employed by functionaries within the state served to exclude the popular masses from

participating in the exercise of state power. See also Mary Kweit and Robert Kweit, "Bureaucratic Decision-Making: Impediments to Citizen Participation," *Polity* 12 (1980), p. 647, for a discussion of the underlying premises of bureaucratic reasoning and how this favours participation by citizen groups that most closely approximate the bureaucrats themselves in terms of values and ideological orientation.

9. For an example of a social movement attempting to develop strategic and tactical resources for dealing with the state, see Clifford Maynes, *Public Consultation: A Citizens Handbook* (Toronto: Ontario Environment Network, 1989). For a discussion of the contradictions involved in engaging in politics on the terrain of the administrative state, see Sophie Watson (ed.), *Playing the State: Australia Feminist Interventions* (London: Verso, 1990).

10. Claus Offe, "Theses on the Welfare State" and "Social Policy and the Theory of the State" in Claus Offe, *Contradictions of the Welfare State* (Cambridge: MIT Press, 1984). For a discussion of how these contradictions have changed the structure of the Canadian state, see Chris Boyle, "The 'Irrationality' of the State: The Nielson Report as a Challenge to Left Analysis," *Studies in Political Economy* 27 (1988), p. 53–85.

11. See Nicos Poulantzas, *State, Power, Socialism,* supra. note 8, p. 91.

12. *Ibid.*

13. See, for example, Boaventura de Sousa Santos, "State, Law and Community in the World System: An Introduction," *Social and Legal Studies* 1 (1992), p. 131–42, and "Law and Community: The Changing Nature of State Power in Late Capitalism," in Richard Abel, (ed.), *The Politics of Informal Justice* (Vol. 1), (New York: Academic Press, 1982), p. 249–66; Sally Merry, "Legal Pluralism," *Law and Society Review* 22 (1988), p. 869–96.

14. Santos, "State, Law and Community," ibid, p. 133.

15. Ibid, p. 133–44.

16. In addition to the citations found in note 6 above, see also Alan Hunt, "Rights and Social Movements: Counter-Hegemonic Strategies," *Journal of Law and Society* 17 (1990), p. 309; Michael McCann and Helena Silverstein, "Social Movements and the American State: Legal Mobilization as a Strategy for Democratization," in Greg Albo, David Langille and Leo Panitch (eds.), *A Different Kind of State? Popular Power and Democratic Administration* (Toronto: Oxford University Press, 1993), p. 131; Stuart Scheingold, "Constitutional Rights and Social Change: Civil Rights in Perspective," in Michael McCann and Gerald Houseman (eds.), *Judging the Constitution, Critical Essays on Judicial Law-Making* (Glenview: Scott, Foresman and Co., 1989); S. Brickey and E. Comack, "The Rule of Law in Social Transformation: Is a Jurisprudence of Insurgency Possible?" *Canadian Journal of Law and Society* 2 (1987), p. 97; Joel Handler, *Social Movements and the Legal System: A Theory of Law Reform and Social Change* (New York: Academic Press, 1978).

17. See in particular, Amy Bartholomew and Alan Hunt, "What's Wrong With Rights?" *Law and Inequality* 9 (1990), p. 1–58, who insist that rights claims,

which do not necessarily require recognition by official state institutions, can be distinguished from legal and constitutional rights, which have received some degree of official sanction. They argue that critics of rights too often focus only on the latter types of rights, thereby restricting themselves to law in the courts.

18. Michael McCann, "Legal Mobilization and Social Reform Movements: Notes on Theory and Its Applications," *Studies in Law, Politics and Soeity* 11 (1991), p. 229–30.

19. This characterization is articulated in Fudge and Glasbeek, "The Politics of Rights," supra. note 1, p. 46–48.

20. For interesting comments on how the new public interest law is sceptical of bureaucracy and state interventions, see Louise Trubek, "Critical Lawyering: Toward a New Public Interest Practice," *Boston University Public Interest Law Journal* 1 (1991), p. 52. This perspective may be contrasted with that of Alan Hutchinson and Andrew Petter, who argue that the danger of rights discourse is that it stands against the state, thereby portraying the state as an enemy from which protection is needed. This, they argue, obscures the state's historic role as ally and protector of the disadvantaged, as witnessed by social welfare interventions. See Alan Hutchinson and Andrew Petter, "The Liberal Lie of the Charter," supra. note 4. See also Andrew Petter, "The Politics of the Charter," *Supreme Court Law Review* 3 (1986), p. 472.

21. A number of other scholars also emphasize the indirect benefits of a litigation strategy. See, for example, Elizabeth Schneider, "The Dialectics of Rights and Politics: Perspectives from the Women's Movement," *New York University Law Review* 61 (1986), p. 589–652; Scheingold, "Constitutional Rights and Social Change," supra. note 16; and Bartholomew and Hunt, "What's Wrong with Rights," supra. note 17.

22. In part, the optimistic approach many pro-rights advocates display towards the legal profession may stem from their own histories as activist lawyers. See, for example, Schneider, ibid. See also some of the "minority positions" within the Critical Legal Studies movement described by Hunt and Bartholomew, supra., note 17, p. 34–49.

23. See Jamie Cassels and Maureen Maloney, "Critical Legal Education: Paralysis with a Purpose," *Canadian Journal of Law and Society* 4 (1990), p. 99. See also Janet Mosher, "Legal Education: Nemesis or Ally of Social Movements," *Osgoode Hall Law Journal* 35 (1997), p. 613–35.

24. Robert Granfield, *Making Elite Lawyers: Visions of Law at Harvard and Beyond* (New York: Routledge, 1992). See also Sherene Razack on the ideological perspectives and orientations of the founding members of the Women's Legal Education and Action Fund. Despite their radicalism, these lawyers tended to display a fundamental acceptance and belief in the existing political system: Sherene Razack, *Canadian Feminism and the Law, the Women's Legal Education and Action Fund and the Pursuit of Equality* (Toronto, Second Story Press, 1991), p. 35. See also Lois Johnson, "The New Public Interest Law:

From Old Theories to a New Agenda," *Boston University Public Interest Law Journal* 1 (1991), p. 173.

25. On the role of professions in monopolizing expertise and knowledge as a market strategy, see Magali Sarfatti Larson, *The Rise of Professionalism: A Sociological Analysis* (Berkeley: University of California Press, 1977).

26. See, for example, Magali Sarfatti Larson, "The Changing Functions of Lawyers in the Liberal State: Reflections for Comparative Analysis," in Richard Abel and Philip Lewis, *Lawyers in Society: Comparative Theories* (Berkeley: University of California Press, 1989).

27. See, for example, Gary Bellow and Jeanne Kettleson, "From Ethics to Politics: Confronting Scarcity and Fairness in Public Interest Practice," *Boston University Law Review* 58(1978), p. 337. Bellow and Kettleson argue that the standards of practice followed within a legal clinic context should be the same as those of the private bar. For a critique of this position, see Paul R. Tremblay, "Toward a Community-Based Ethic for Legal Services Practice," *UCLA Law Review* 37 (1990), p. 1101.

28. Robert L. Nelson and David M. Trubek, "Arenas of Professionalism: The Professional Ideologies of Lawyers in Context," in Robert Nelson, David Trubek and Rayman Solomon (eds.), *Lawyers' Ideals/Lawyers' Practices: Transformations in the American Legal Profession* (Ithaca: Cornell University Press, 1992), p. 179.

29. See Pierre Bourdieu, "The Force of Law: Toward a Sociology of the Juridical Field," *The Hastings Law Journal* 38 (1987), p. 818.

30. B. Sheldrick, "Law, Representation, and Political Activism: Community-based Practice and the Mobilization of Legal Resources," *Canadian Journal of Law and Society* 10 (1995), p. 155–84.

31. On the Northwestern Experiment, see Robert Granfield, supra. note 24. See also the Web site for the People's Law School in British Columbia: <www.publiclegaled.bc.ca>.

32. Austin Sarat and Stuart Scheingold, "Cause Lawyering and the Reproduction of Professional Authority," in Austin Sarat and Stuart Scheingold (eds.), *Cause Lawyering: Political Commitments and Professional Responsibilities* (Oxford: Oxford University Press, 1998), p. 5.

Chapter 3

Regulating Dissent

It may seem counter-intuitive to say that law can play an important part in an activist strategy. Law generally is a system of rules designed to secure and maintain the existing social order, rather than a vehicle for social transformation. The Ontario Coalition Against Poverty (OCAP), in its guide to law for activists, takes the position that the law is primarily designed for the "containment of the poor," "the protection of property" and the "replication of the social order."[1] This is certainly true. It is also true that the law plays a very important role in regulating and controlling dissent. Protests, demonstrations, strikes and acts of civil disobedience are all circumscribed by a host of legal rules and regulations that can blunt and limit their impact.

Controlling Dissent

Outright prohibition of dissent has rarely been successful in western democracies. Banning and criminalizing dissent requires a level of repression that is generally considered unacceptable in liberal democracies. This is not to say that efforts have not been made to achieve this result and that the use of the state's coercive power—most often by the police but also, on occasion, by the military—has not and does not occur. Striking workers, anti-globalization demonstrators and Aboriginal activists, to name a few, can certainly attest to the willingness of the state to use repression.

Generally the liberal democratic state permits attempts to control dissent rather than suppress it outright. The constitutional protection of the rights of free speech and peaceful assembly make it difficult to prohibit demonstrations and other forms of political expression. Instead, the state uses its regulatory power to contain dissent and regulate it both bureaucratically and through the police.

The history of the labour movement provides an important example of this tendency. At the turn of the century, labour unions were considered illegal organizations. Legislators and employers saw unions as an illegal restraint on trade that prevented employers from negotiating individual employment contracts with their workers. This legal position led to a series of violent and disruptive strikes in which trade unions sought to force employers to recognize and accept the union as the workers' bargaining agent. Eventually, labour peace was secured through state intervention acknowledging the right of unions to exist and bargain for workers, and instituting regulatory processes that limit and constrain the right to strike.[2]

In particular, strikes are usually prohibited during the life of a collective agreement. The timing and duration of strikes are often subject to legislative control. Strikes are only permissible after good faith bargaining has taken place and in some instances after a period of state-supervised conciliation or mediation. Workers in employment sectors deemed "essential"—such as health care, policing and teaching—are frequently denied the right to strike. Wildcat or illegal strikes—strikes while a collective agreement is in force—can result in union leaders being jailed and/or fined. In some instances, they may even lead to dismissal.[3]

Even where a strike is legal, the actual conduct of the strike may be subject to various forms of regulation. Legislation may prescribe the number of picketers permitted at any particular location, or it may provide that entry and exit from the workplace cannot be disrupted. Striking workers are not allowed on company property, and in many instances secondary picketing is prohibited.[4] If the various rules of picketing are not complied with, or if any other laws are violated, the police and the courts enforce compliance. Employers may seek injunctions to prohibit or limit picketing; they may also apply to a labour board for an order forcing the union to comply with labour legislation.[5] If picket line violence occurs, property is damaged or any court orders are not complied with, the police may make arrests. In short, striking has been transformed from a political action to a much more regulated stage of the bargaining process.[6]

The regulation of strikes represents a highly developed system governing the expression of dissension by workers. Most other forms of demonstration and protest, while not so heavily monitored, are nonetheless subject to important forms of regulation and control. The control of dissent involves a number of different levels of government and includes municipalities, as well as provincial/state governments and central governments.

At the local level, the organizers of demonstrations may need to comply with municipal land use and traffic bylaws. An event planned in a local park may require a permit. If entertainment is going to be provided, local regulations again may require a permit, while noise bylaws may justify the police shutting down the event if proper approvals have not been obtained. Many demonstrations involve some sort of march or parade. The march is a good vehicle for spreading the group's message. Disrupting traffic ensures that the event is noticed and travelling from one location to another means the message is communicated to people who might otherwise not be reached. Most municipalities, however, prohibit parades on city streets without prior approval of either the police department or some other local official.

City bylaws frequently define a parade in very broad terms. Bylaws in Canada typically define a parade as any group of "pedestrians numbering more than 30 that are standing, marching or walking anywhere on a street or sidewalk or any group of vehicles numbering

> ### Regulating the Form of Protest
>
> In 1982 the Community for Creative Non-Violence received a permit from the American National Park Service to hold a demonstration in Lafayette Park and the Mall, two national parks in the heart of Washington D.C. The purpose of the demonstrations was to raise awareness of the issue of homelessness. While the permit allowed the erection of two symbolic tent cities, protesters were prohibited from sleeping overnight in the tents on the grounds that this violated Park Service rules about camping in undesignated campsites. A challenge to this restriction was dismissed by the U.S. Supreme Court on the ground that the Park Service was justified in regulating the time, place and manner in which the demonstration was conducted.
>
> *Clark v. Community for Creative Nonviolence*, 468 U.S. 288 (1984).

more than 10 that are stopped or moving anywhere on a street."[7] Such bylaws typically exclude the armed forces and funeral processions. Organizers need to apply in writing to the police department for permission prior to the parade. Different jurisdictions require different notice periods, but applications must be made anywhere from 48 hours to 90 days in advance of the event. The longer the time period, the more difficult it is to mount spontaneous demonstrations or to respond quickly to public issues through the organization of a demonstration or march.

The application process generally requires that the individuals organizing the parade stipulate in writing the starting time of the parade, how long it is going to last, the specific route and the location of formation and dispersal of the marchers. The organizers may also have to pay a fee as well as any additional money required by the police for the purpose of publishing notices of the parade and diverting traffic. The police department often has a relatively unfettered discretion to approve or deny an application for a parade. However, it should be noted that this discretion does have to be exercised in light of constitutional rights to free expression. In the United States, for example, this has led to a significant legal doctrine about the contexts in which parade permits can be denied. Generally speaking, the content of the marcher's message is an insufficient ground for denying a permit.[8] In other words, the denial must be based on something other than the fact that local authorities do not like the group or what it has to say.

The police department, however, can issue a permit subject to a variety of conditions. In particular, the local authorities may change or restrict the route, the timing and the manner of organization and marshalling of the parade. Deviation from any conditions contained in the permit leads to its nullification, thereby rendering the march illegal. The permit process, then, gives local authorities the opportunity to regulate protest marchers. Authorities frequently utilize the permit process to engage in a dialogue with the organizers of a march. It is a chance to secure the consent and compliance of the group, thereby minimizing the potential for problems. The requirement that all permit conditions be strictly adhered to, which is frequently impossible, also gives the police the opportunity to shut down the parade if they choose. Local regulations, then, give the authorities a choice as to how they regulate demonstrations, either through the strict enforcement of rules and the use of force, or through a more negotiated and managed process.

In addition to local regulation of marches and demonstrations, protesters may find themselves subject to a number of criminal and quasi-criminal regulations. The rules of trespass, for example, may prevent demonstrations and events from being held on private property. In the United Kingdom, trespass rules have been extended to include common land that previously was open to all members of the public. Moreover, under the terms of the British *Criminal Justice and Public Order Act* of 1994, several changes were made to public order legislation that effectively transforms trespass from a civil wrong to an act with criminal consequences.[9] This means that once individuals are requested to leave by local authorities and fail to do so, they may be arrested and charged, possibly facing fines or imprisonment.[10]

Other criminal offences that individuals participating in a demonstration may find themselves subject to include a wide range of offences. Some of these are fairly minor, such as causing a disturbance, while others, such as assault, obstruction of police or damaging property are more serious. Obviously the degree to which a participant will be exposed to charges for these things depends on the individual's own level of participation, the nature and purpose of the demonstration and whether the police are strictly enforcing the law or are willing to overlook some breaches of law.

Most demonstrations provide ample opportunity for the police to lay charges. Of course, this does not mean that the charges are justified or that convictions will result. Nevertheless arrests, however unjustified, serve as a tool for forcing demonstrators to disperse and for removing the leadership of the demonstration. It should also be noted that historically courts have not always been sympathetic to demonstrators. Striking workers, for example, have been convicted of mischief to property for pasting posters onto mailboxes and for "denting" vehicles transporting replacement workers by kicking them as they passed through

> **Reading the Riot Act**
>
> Illegal activity by some protestors may result in the entire demonstration being declared illegal. In July 2003, anti-globalization activists organized a march and demonstration protesting the World Trade Organization, which was holding meetings in Montreal. Although the majority of demonstrators were peaceful, pockets of violence and vandalism led the police to declare the entire gathering illegal. The police ordered the demonstrators to disperse by "reading the riot act." Anyone failing to do so could then be arrested for participating in an illegal demonstration. Police arrested over 200 people.

the picket line. A coalition of global justice activists organized at the 1977 meetings of the Asia–Pacific Economic Cooperation (APEC) in Vancouver. At those protests, one of the leaders, Jaggi Singh, was arrested for "assaulting a police officer" by speaking too loudly near the officer's ear with a megaphone. In 2001, during demonstrations against the Free Trade Area of the Americas (FTAA) in Quebec City, Singh was again arrested, for possession of a dangerous weapon: a catapult designed to throw teddy bears over the temporary wall surrounding the FTAA meeting site. That Singh was acquitted of these charges does not take away from the fact that the police were able to use their arrest power to remove him from the action.

Activists have developed a number of strategies for dealing with the potential for arrest.[11] Often a legal team organizes prior to the event. This may involve securing the assistance of lawyers or paralegals sympathetic to the cause and willing to help represent those arrested. The phone numbers of people who can arrange legal representation may be distributed or even be written in ink by activists on their bodies to ensure ease of access. If trouble is anticipated, individuals may arrange in advance to provide bail or a surety to secure release from jail.[12]

Some individuals may be given the responsibility of documenting the event, either through the service of independent media videographers or by taking notes. This can be useful for keeping track of who is arrested but also for documenting what took place prior to arrest and police behaviour during the demonstration. It should be noted, however, that videotapes of material can only be admitted into evidence in court if certain conditions are met. First, the individual who actually took the video will usually be required to appear before the court to testify as to how and when it was made and to verify that there has been no editing or alteration of the footage. It is also important to remember that the entire video or roll of film will have to be admitted into evidence. This means that both those parts of the video that might be helpful to activists (exculpatory) and those that might be harmful to their cause (inculpatory) will be viewed by the court. Video footage, therefore, may turn out to be evidence against activists. It may also be the case that the police seize tapes and video made by activists or members of the independent media. Generally there are fairly strict rules regarding the search and seizure of media outlets. However, it is not at all clear that the courts will extend the same protections to independent media outlets, which are often small scale and appear to operate on a more individual or amateur basis. If the producers of the video have links to the movement that engaged in the demonstration, the court may also conclude that they are not part of the "objective" news-gathering media, but rather partisan participants in the demonstration itself. These factors may mean that police will have an easier time securing search warrants for independent media videographers than they would have if they were trying to seize tapes made by an "official" news organization.

Despite the many resources at the disposal of the authorities to arrest and detain demonstrators, there has been a general trend over the past two decades away from a strict and confrontational approach to policing demonstrations. A number of commentators note a shift in police practices from a position of "escalating force" to one dominated by the "negotiated management of demonstrations."[13] The former approach, which dominated policing of demonstrations in both North America and Europe during the 1960s and 1970s, was characterized by a general intolerance of political dissent and its expression. Police were unsympathetic to demonstrators' rights to free expression, were willing to use force and arrests to prevent demonstrations, and engaged in very little dialogue with the organizers of actions. As a result, civil rights and anti-Vietnam war demonstrations in the United States and student and labour demonstrations in Europe during that period were characterized as a series of violent confrontations.[14]

This approach has increasingly been replaced by police strategies that are more respectful of demonstrators' rights, yet designed to reduce the impact of mass actions. Authorities are more willing to permit demonstrations and overlook minor infractions of the law, and may try to avoid confrontations with demonstrators. At the same time, police utilize the approvals process to ensure that demonstrations create the minimum disruption possible and that their political significance is muted. This is done by routing parades and marches into areas of the city where there will be fewer spectators, less likelihood of confrontation and less disruption to traffic and commerce. As a result, the message of the group, while permitted to be expressed, is generally blunted. This was certainly the situation in Vancouver during the 1997 APEC conference. Demonstrators protesting the presence of Indonesian President Suharto, while allowed on the University of British Columbia campus where the meetings were taking place, were nevertheless not permitted to demonstrate in close proximity to the meeting site. As a result, the political leaders and delegates to the conference were generally unaware of the demonstrations.[15]

Application of negotiated management strategies to demonstrations has always been selective. The law provides the police with the resources necessary to take a hard line with demonstrators, either by denying the right to demonstrate completely or by strictly applying the law during a demonstration and using force and arrests to control demonstrators. Failure to comply with police directives during a march or demonstration, for example, can result in arrests for obstructing the police. While charges are often never pursued in court, nevertheless, the use of arrests can effectively bring an end to the political action. The police tend to be far less sympathetic and tolerant, and violent incidents therefore more likely to occur, in cases where demonstrators are perceived to be "subversive, unpatriotic, or communistic" and where their activities embarrass the government.[16] In these situations, the softer, more managerial approach to protest is frequently set aside. This tendency was also evident at the APEC demonstrations in Vancouver. While the initial police strategy was to confine and contain demonstrators, once they had refused to comply with the restrictions, force, including the use of pepper spray, was readily employed by the police.[17]

The experience of the anti–globalization movement seems to confirm this. Authorities have responded to the movement's growing militancy with a more aggressive approach to policing. This has included the targeting of the movement's leadership for arrest and detention, the construction of an impenetrable barricade at the Free Trade Area of the Americas summit in Quebec City, the use of tear gas, water cannons and rubber bullets to control demonstrators, and in Genoa, the killing of one demonstrator. The police insist that such measures are necessary to ensure the security of political leaders and the general public and to prevent

militant elements of the movement from damaging property and inter-
rupting the meetings. Nevertheless, the failure of the police to prevent
demonstrators from disrupting the World Trade Organization meetings in
the "Battle of Seattle" led many to view the anti-globalization demonstrations as a significant threat to domestic security, and activists as deliberately
seeking to break the law and incite riots. The police have responded by
returning to an "escalating force" approach to policing these demonstrations.

The Royal Canadian Mounted Police (RCMP) have established a
"public order program" to help the force develop and exchange intelligence and information for the policing of demonstrations. This includes
increased training on how to control demonstrations and how to make use
of "non-lethal defensive tools" such as pepper spray, rubber bullets and
tear gas.[18] In addition, in a move many consider to be a form of
harassment, RCMP and Canadian Security Intelligence Service (CSIS)
agents have begun to visit activists prior to demonstrations. Moreover,
these visits have been made not only to activists with a history of violence
but to a wide range of organizations and individuals with no association
with violent organizations.[19]

The RCMP and CSIS have also increased intelligence gathering on
activist organizations and conducted "threat assessments" of a large
number of groups. Prior to the APEC meetings, threat assessments were
conducted on the National Council of Catholic Women, Catholic
Charities USA, Greenpeace, Amnesty International, the Canadian Council of Churches, the Council of Canadians and the International Centre
for Human Rights and Democratic Development.[20] After the Quebec
City demonstrations, CSIS advised Parliament that violent fringe groups of
the anti-globalization movement, such as the Black Bloc, as well as
militant factions of the animal rights and environmental groups were
showing up at anti-globalization protests and were potential security
threats.[21]

Anti-Terrorism and Dissent

The move by authorities towards a more repressive approach to demonstrations has intensified since the terrorist attacks on the Pentagon and the
World Trade Center in New York. The concern about terrorism, and the
preoccupation of many western democracies with security, has led to
greater scrutiny and tighter controls on demonstrations and protests.
Certainly the police and security forces have been given wide-ranging and
new powers to deal with security issues. Many of these powers can be

utilized to target dissidents and activists in social movements. The language of terrorism has been applied to activists. The chief of Toronto's police, for example, has referred to OCAP activities as examples of domestic terrorism. Recent demonstrations throughout North America and Europe to protest the American and British attack on Iraq were closely policed, with arrests and force used to quell demonstrators.[22]

Anti-terrorism legislation that has been enacted since Sept. 11, 2001, increases police powers, not only to gather intelligence information on dissidents, but also to arrest and detain those suspected of "terrorist activity." Significant new legislation has been enacted in a variety of jurisdictions. The United States' *Patriot Act*, for example, represents a significant expansion of police powers to engage in the surveillance of terrorist suspects.[23] Similarly, the United Kingdom's *Terrorist Act* expands the powers of the police to investigate alleged terrorist activities, but also to stop and search individuals and vehicles, and provides for the detention of suspects after arrest for up to seven days before charges must be laid.[24]

The difficulty with much of this legislation is that the definition of terrorism is so broad that a wide range of dissident activities might be included within its scope. The extent of the expansion of police powers is well demonstrated by the Canadian response to the threat of terrorism. Very shortly after the events of September 11, 2001 the federal government enacted Bill C-36, the *Anti-Terrorism Act*. The Act greatly expands police powers, permitting preventative arrests of those suspected of terrorist activities and suspending the usual rules against self-incrimination. Individuals can be required to answer questions put to them and refusal can lead to imprisonment.[25]

The definition of terrorist activity in the Act is quite broad and could potentially cover many forms of political protest and expression. Bill C-36 defines a terrorist act as "an act or omission committed for political, religious or ideological purposes." There must also be an intention to either intimidate the public regarding security, including economic security, or to compel a person, government, or domestic or international organization to do something. In addition, the activity must also intentionally

- cause death or serious bodily harm;
- endanger life;
- cause a serious risk to health or safety of the public or any segment of the public;

- cause substantial public or private property damage that is also likely to disrupt an essential service intending to cause a serious risk to health or safety of the public; or
- cause serious interference with or serious disruption of an essential service, facility or system whether public or private.

The Act defines a terrorist group as any organization that has as one of its purposes or activities the facilitation or carrying out of any terrorist activity. It also makes it an offence to participate in a terrorist activity. Moreover, it is possible to be convicted of this offence regardless of whether the activity is actually carried out, the individual's participation actually aided in the carrying out of the activity or the individual had any actual knowledge about the activity. The Act also criminalizes the financing of terrorist activities and the facilitation of terrorist activities.

The definition of terrorist activity could easily apply to the practices of many political groups. They act for ideological reasons, and the notion of intimidating the public, especially with respect to economic security, is a very broad and elastic concept. Moreover, many groups specifically aim to disrupt services as part of conveying their message. The legislation excludes disruptions of services as a result of "lawful" advocacy, protest, dissent or a stoppage of work that is not intended to cause death or serious bodily harm, endanger a person's life or be a substantial risk to the public's health or safety.

No one can object to legislation that actually targets and seeks to punish genuine terrorists. There's concern, however, that the vagueness of the definition of "terrorist activity" could well lead to the targeting of dissidents and political activists who are unpopular or who engage in tactics that include a degree of civil disobedience. It could also lead to the prosecution of individuals who organize demonstrations where violence or property damage occurs, even where organizers planned a peaceful event.

The exemption for protest and advocacy is limited by the word "lawful." Civil disobedience, including many of the tactics routinely used by environmental activists and other groups, would be considered unlawful and therefore not fall within this exemption: for example, blockading a highway, chaining oneself to a tree, or holding a protest march without a permit. Although they are frequently tolerated by the police, they could be deemed "terrorist" activities. They are certainly designed to compel the government to engage in a particular course of action. If they have the effect of disrupting services, endangering the physical safety of people or causing damage to property, then legitimate protest might be reclassified as a terrorist activity.

It is also possible that the presence of some violent segments within a protest demonstration might lead the authorities to classify peaceful activists as a potential threat or as individuals participating in a terrorist activity. The Act provides some guidance for determining whether someone has actually participated in the activity of a terrorist group. This includes such things as whether the person has used the words or symbols associated with the group, whether they frequently associate with members of the group, and whether they engage in activities at the instruction of any person in the terrorist group. It is quite possible that carrying a banner or placard, or publishing and/or distributing brochures and pamphlets articulating an anti-globalization message might be sufficient to bring someone within the scope of this section. Similarly, attending meetings or protests, or aiding in the planning of a protest or demonstration might constitute a sufficient association with a group to brand someone as participating in a "terrorist organization."

In addition, Canada has also enacted Bill C-35, the *Foreign Missions and International Organizations Act*.[26] This legislation was primarily a response to the anti-globalization protests that took place in Quebec City in 2000. It expands the definition of an "internationally protected person" and extends diplomatic immunity to representatives of foreign states participating in international organizations. Members of the individual's family and household are also included. An international organization, for the purposes of the legislation, can include a host of non-governmental organizations and intergovernmental conferences such as the G8, the Summit of the Americas and a variety of other trade summits and international gatherings. Significantly, the legislation was passed just prior to the G8 meetings at Kananaskis in June 2002.

The Act protects not only the physical well-being of the individuals covered by it, but also their "freedom" or "dignity." This clearly raises the possibility of the police using these powers to restrict legitimate dissent. At the APEC demonstrations in Vancouver, demonstrators were not allowed to get close to the meetings because of government's concern that President Suharto of Indonesia would be offended. The authorities might have considered the demonstrations an attack on Suharto's "dignity," thereby justifying the arrest and detention of protesters. It is also an offence to attack the means of transportation of an internationally protected person.[27] While this section would clearly apply to physical attacks, there is no obvious reason it could not be applied to attempts to blockade transportation routes and prevent delegates to a trade summit from reaching the meeting site.

Bill C-35 also gives the RCMP the authority to provide security at international conferences and to control, limit or prohibit access to any area "to the extent and in a manner that is reasonable in the circumstances." This clearly gives the RCMP the authority to prohibit individuals from entering areas in proximity to an international meeting. It might even give the police the authority to order an individual to leave the city where a conference is taking place. How broad a power this entails depends on the interpretation of the phrase "reasonable in the circumstances." However, this is a fairly broad and ambiguous limitation and the courts may be reluctant to second-guess the authorities on the design and implementation of security arrangements.

While the government insists these laws are not intended to stifle dissent and legitimate political activity, there is considerable evidence to suggest that the authorities have used their expanded power to target activists. A recent report by the International Civil Liberties Monitoring Group, a coalition of NGOs concerned with human rights, indicates that the enactment of anti-terrorism legislation has contributed to the criminalization of political dissent.[28]

The report states that, in September 2002, Bill C-36 was formally invoked by the RCMP and CSIS to obtain a search warrant and conduct a raid on the residence of two Aboriginal activists in British Columbia. The raid was carried out by an Integrated National Security Team (INSET), a series of groups created under Bill C-36 to allow better coordination between the RCMP, CSIS and local police forces. The raid was reportedly to search for weapons, although no illegal weapons were found and no charges were laid. The information used to obtain the search warrant has been sealed and, consequently, cannot be scrutinized. A CSIS briefing document prepared for the Solicitor General in November 2002 indicated that while the agency's top security concern was al-Qaeda, elements of the anti-globalization movement were an ongoing security concern and authorities should take "extraordinary caution" to prevent trouble at international conferences.[29]

While there is no doubt that the international security climate was significantly altered by the events of September 11, the new anti-terrorist legislation has dramatically increased police powers to engage in the surveillance of activists and to intervene in lawful political protest. The police and intelligence services have always displayed considerable antipathy towards activists, frequently seeking to create state enemies and security threats out of political dissent.[30] The new anti-terrorism measures give the authorities even greater tools to do this.

SLAPPs: The Private Attack on Dissent

It is not always the state that is involved in suppressing dissent. In some instances private corporations also take steps to curb and restrict the expression of political activism. Corporations and governments have found that suing activists and protesters, as a form of pre-emptive strike, can be an effective mechanism to constrain and limit their activities. Lawsuits of this sort are frequently brought against individuals and community groups that oppose corporations and governments on issues of public concern. Such litigation has come to be called SLAPPs—strategic litigation against public participation.[31] Although most SLAPPs are ulti-mately unsuccessful, they have the effect of forcing activists to divert time and resources to defending themselves against the litigation. Regardless of the outcome of such cases, the drain on resources can cause a group to stop its activities. More broadly, the threat of SLAPP can create a chill on public involvement in important public issues that extends beyond those who are actually sued. corporations

SLAPP lawsuits have been brought for a wide range of legitimate political activities. These include:

- writing a "letter to the editor";
- circulating petitions;
- contacting a public official;
- reporting police misconduct;
- erecting a sign or displaying a banner on one's property;
- complaining to school officials about teacher misconduct or unsafe conditions in a school;
- speaking at a public meeting;
- reporting unlawful activities;
- testifying before legislative committees;
- speaking out as a representative of a public interest group;
- filing a public interest lawsuit; and
- giving interviews to the media.[32]

SLAPP generally takes the form of a civil lawsuit alleging that the activities of protesters have somehow caused the private corporation or government official some damage or injury. As a result, the SLAPP diverts attention and resources away from the "real" public issue to collateral or

The McLibel Case

Helen Steel, a gardener, and Dave Morris, a local postman, were members of Greenpeace and had participated in demonstrations outside McDonald's restaurants in London, England. After distributing pamphlets entitled "What's Wrong With McDonald's?—Everything they don't want you to know," they were sued for libel by McDonald's. The pamphlets attacked almost every aspect of the McDonald's business operations. In particular, they accused the restaurant chain of exploiting children through their advertising, promoting unhealthy diets, exploiting their employees, damaging the environment and mistreating animals. The trial lasted two and a half years and Steel and Morris defended themselves. Legal aid in the United Kingdom is unavailable for libel cases. In the end, although the judge accepted the truth of many of the statements contained in the pamphlet, Steel and Morris were unable to demonstrate the truth of all of the allegations. As a result, the libel case was successful and the pair were ordered to pay £60,000 in damages. They refused and McDonald's eventually abandoned the case. Given that Steel and Morris had no assets whatsoever, McDonald's would never have been able to collect the damage award and had little choice but to give up. The full story of the McLibel case can be found at the McSpotlight Website: <www.mcspotlight.org>.

lost cause

ancillary issues of any damage suffered by the plaintiff. The most common grounds of injury alleged in SLAPP lawsuits include the following.[33]

Defamation: This is an intentionally false communication, which is either published (libel) or spoken publicly (slander), and which injures an individual or a corporation's reputation. This was the basis of the "McLibel" lawsuit in which activists Helen Steel and Dave Morris were sued by McDonald's in 1994 for distributing pamphlets outside a McDonald's restaurant in London England.

Invasion of Privacy/Exploitation of Personality: This involves using images of an individual or publishing an individual's private affairs without consent. Showing an individual's image on pamphlets and materials distributed by a group, or even on placards used during a demonstration, might lead to this action.

Malicious Prosecution or Abuse of Process: A civil or criminal lawsuit may constitute a malicious prosecution if it was known that there was no merit in the case and it was brought to harass or persecute the defendants. Corporations and individuals have argued that launching a public interest lawsuit constitutes a malicious prosecution. It is extremely difficult to make a case for malicious prosecution, which is one reason activists unjustly charged by the police rarely seek redress. However, from the point of view of a corporation with plenty of resources, there is little to be lost by bringing a case forward. Ironically, many SLAPPs themselves could be considered abuses of process.

Conspiracy: A conspiracy is an agreement between two or more persons to commit an illegal, unlawful or wrongful act. An agreement to hold an illegal demonstration or to engage in civil disobedience might give rise to this sort of charge.

Interference with Contract or Economic Advantage: This involves a situation where activists do something that interferes with a corporation's or an individual's ability to carry out their business dealings. For example, environmentalists or Aboriginal groups blockading a logging road may interfere with the logging company's ability to honour supply contracts. SLAPPs alleging interference with economic activity have also been brought in response to boycott campaigns.

Intentional Infliction of Emotional Distress: This involves the commission of an act intended to cause severe mental or emotional anguish to another person. (It may come as a surprise to many activists just how sensitive corporate presidents and government officials can be.)

Nuisance: This is a very broad category of claims. It involves anything that obstructs the use and enjoyment of property, but also applies to actions that endanger, or potentially endanger life or health, give offence to the senses, or violate the laws of decency. Blockades, sit-ins or graffiti spray painted on walls could potentially give rise to this sort of claim.

Injunction: An injunction is actually a remedy rather than a cause of action. Many SLAPPs seek either a permanent or temporary order requiring activists to stop their activities. Failure to comply with an injunction constitutes contempt of court and can lead to a fine or imprisonment. In many instances, the plaintiff in a SLAPP case will ask for an "interlocutory injunction." This is an injunction that is requested prior to the actual conclusion of the litigation and determination of whether or not the plaintiff's claim has any merit. In many instances, the interlocutory injunction is really what the plaintiff is after, because once the main issue comes up for trial the political battle may already be over.

Activists have begun to muster resources to fight back against SLAPP litigation. Resources have been mobilized and made available to groups and individuals exposed to SLAPPs. In California, for example, activists created the Anti-SLAPP Project, which provides both information and advice to individuals, groups and lawyers.[34] Since SLAPPs effectively constrain the enjoyment of constitutionally protected rights to freedom of expression, pressure has been brought on legislators to curb SLAPPs. A number of American states have enacted anti-SLAPP legislation. This legislation usually enables defendants in SLAPP cases to make a special motion to the court to have the statement of claim struck out. The legislation provides that the cause of action should be struck out if it was brought as a result of an individual exercising her rights of free speech. For the case to continue, the plaintiffs must show that there is a reasonable probability they will be successful at trial. Given that most SLAPP cases are spurious, this will frequently be difficult. The legislation provides a relatively expeditious and inexpensive mechanism for resolving most SLAPP cases and preventing the plaintiff from using the SLAPP as a vehicle to harass and persecute social action groups and individuals for their involvement in public affairs.

In Canada, the only jurisdiction to pass anti-SLAPP legislation was British Columbia under the New Democratic Party.[35] That legislation, which was passed in 2001, followed the general format described above, but was broader in some important respects. It permitted SLAPP defendants to go before the court and have a proceeding dismissed on the grounds that it had been brought for an "improper purpose." An improper purpose was defined by the legislation as including dissuading someone from engaging in public participation, diverting the defendant's resources from public participation to the proceedings, or penalizing the defendant for engaging in public participation. Public participation was, in turn, defined as any communication or conduct aimed at influencing public opinion or promoting or furthering lawful action by the public or any government body in relation to a matter of public interest. Unfortunately, this legislation was one of the last acts of the New Democratic government before its defeat in 2001. The subsequent Liberal government of Gordon Campbell has adopted an extreme neo-liberal, pro-business agenda. As a result, the *Protection of Public Participation Act* was repealed in its entirety on August 16, 2001, a mere four and a half months after being enacted.

One of the best ways for a group to protect against a SLAPP is to ensure that everything it prints or says can be justified and supported. Good research and proper documentation are essential. The best defence against a defamation suit is to prove that what you said is true. The importance of good documentation is well demonstrated by the Friends of the Lubicon case. A volunteer group opposed to logging on the traditional lands of the Lubicon Cree Nation in northern Alberta was sued in 1998 by Daishowa, a multinational paper company. The company claimed damages as a result of an effective campaign to boycott products manufactured by the company. The suit was eventually overturned and the court ruled that the boycott and protests were legal. Daishowa appealed, but eventually it abandoned its appeal in May 2000. In part, the Friends of the Lubicon were successful because they were very careful to ensure that everything they published was backed up by careful research. It was also useful that the material they published gave both sides of the story, allowing individuals to make up their own minds as to which arguments to accept.[36]

Dissent, Control and Rights

There are a number of mechanisms through which the state and private corporations can restrict dissent by activists. Authorities may try to control and direct the expression of dissent through permits and regulations, or they may try to close off avenues of dissent completely. The so-called "War on Terror" has provided authorities with new tools for both maintaining surveillance of activists, and arresting and detaining them. Of course, the capacity of the state to restrict dissent raises serious issues of human rights and civil liberties. In some instances, activists will choose to resist state efforts to restrict dissent using constitutional arguments about freedom of expression and freedom of assembly. In other instances, asserting rights-based arguments may, in itself, be a vehicle for expressing dissent and advancing a political cause. Appealing to rights raises a number of tactical and strategic issues, such as integrating a court challenge into the broader political agenda of the group, dealing with the media, mobilizing members, and raising money and resources for the court case. It is these issues to which I now turn.

Notes

1. Ontario Coalition Against Poverty, *In the Streets and in the Courts—We Fight to Win: A Legal Guide for Activists* (Sept. 2001), ch. 1, "The Police and the State." <www.ocap.ca/archive/legalguide/policestate.htm>.
2. For a discussion of this period in Canada, see Errol Black and Jim Silver, *Building a Better World: An Introduction to Trade Unionism in Canada* (Halifax: Fernwood, 2001). See also Craig Heron, *The Canadian Labour Movement: A Short History* (Toronto: J. Lorimer, 1996).
3. Restrictions on the right to strike in the public sector have been well documented by Leo Panitch and Donald Swartz, *From Consent to Coercion: The Assault on Trade Union Freedoms*, 3rd edition. (Toronto: Garamond Press, 2003).

4. Secondary picketing involves picketing an industry or agency other than the company against which the workers are on strike. In some instances it may be a useful strategy, particularly given the decentralized production processes often employed by modern companies, to picket other enterprises that do business with or provide supplies to the company being "struck."

5. Of course, where the employer violates labour legislation, it is also possible for the union to apply to a labour board for a remedy.

6. Bob Russell, "Social Movements in Practice: Reinventing a Labour Movement?" in William Carroll (ed.), *Organizing Dissent: Contemporary Social Movements in Theory and Practice* (Toronto: Garamond Press, 1997).

7. See City of Winnipeg, Traffic Bylaw no. 1563/77, s.2; and City of Vancouver Traffic Bylaw, s. 99(1).

8. See *Forsyth County, Ga. v. Nationalist Movement* (1992) 515 U.S. 123 (United States Supreme Court).

9. Martin Wasik and Richard Taylor, *Blackstone's Guide to the Criminal Justice and Public Order Act 1994* (London: Blackstone Press, 1995), ch. 4.

10. *Criminal Justice and Public Order Act*, 1994, s. 61(7).

11. These strategies are well documented in OCAP's legal guide for activists. See above, supra. note 1.

12. The posting of bail is a common practice in the United States, where one must actually pay money to secure release on bail. On the other hand, a surety, which is more common in Canada, involves having an individual pledge to pay a certain amount of money should the individual not appear for trial. The surety usually does not require payment up front.

13. Clark McPhail, David Schweingruber and John McCarthy, "Policing Protest in the United States: 1960–1995," in Donatella della Porta and Herbert Reiter (eds.), *Policing Protest: The Control of Mass Demonstrations in Western Democracies* (Minneapolis: University of Minnesota Press, 1998), p. 49–69.

14. Ibid. See also Olivier Fillieule and Fabien Jobard, "The Policing of Protest in France: Toward a Model of Protest Policing," and P.A.J. Waddington, "Controlling Protest in Contemporary Historical and Comparative Perspective," both in della Porta and Reiter, ibid.

15. This has certainly been the experience in the United States. See, for example, McPhail, Schweingruber and McCarthy's discussion of the operation of the Public Order Management system in Washington, DC, supra. note 12. See also Robert Reiner, "Policing, Protest and Disorder in Britain," in Della Porta and Reiter, *Policing Protest*, ibid. For a discussion of the APEC demonstrations, see Wes Pue (ed.), *Pepper in Our Eyes: The APEC Affair* (Vancouver: UBC Press, 2000) and Karen Pearlston, "APEC Days at UBC: Student Protests and National Security in an Era of Trade Liberalization," in Gary Kinsman, Dieter Buse and Mercedes Steedman (eds.), *Whose National Security? Canadian State Surveillance and the Creation of Enemies* (Toronto: Between the Lines Press, 2000).

16. Donatella della Porta and Herbert Reiter, "The Policing of Protest in Western Democracies," in della Porta and Reiter, ibid, p. 20.

17. The use of police force at the APEC demonstrations was found to be excessive by the Commission of Inquiry into police handling of the demonstrations. See *Final Report of the RCMP Police Complaints Commission*, available at <www.cpc-cpp.gc.ca/ePub/APEC/eFinalApec.pdf>.

18. David Pugliese and Jim Bronskill, "Keeping the Public in Check: Special Mountie Team, Police Tactics Threaten the Right to Free Speech and Assembly," *Ottawa Citizen*, August 18, 2001, p. A1.

19. David Pugliese and Jim Bronskill, "How Police Deter Dissent: Government Critics Decry Intimidation," *Ottawa Citizen*, August 21, 2001, p. A1.

20. David Pugliese and Jim Bronskill, supra. note 18, p. A1.

21. Stewart Bell, "CSIS Paints Anti-trade Movement as Menace: Top-Secret Report Warns of 'Violent and Extreme' Elements," *National Post*, Feb. 24, 2003, p. A1.

22. Duncan Campbell, "Forty Injured as Police Fire Rubber Bullets at Peace Protesters," *The Guardian*, April 8, 2003, <www.guardian.co.uk/antiwar/sotry/0,12809,932145,00.html>; "Thousands Join Anti-War Demos," *Guardian Unlimited*, March 23, 2003, <www.guardina.co.uk/antiwar/story/0,12809,919813,00.html>; "Pupils Prominent in Global Anti-War Marches," *Guardian Unlimited*, March 24, 2003, <www.guardian.co.uk/antiwar/story/0,12809,920898,00.html>.

23. *Patriot Act*, P: 2001, 107–56.

24. *Terrorist Act* 2000, chapter 11. This legislation was actually enacted prior to the events of September 11, 2001. The U.K. later enacted a second piece of legislation, the *Anti-Terrorism, Crime and Security Act* 2001, chapter 24.

25. For a discussion of the legal implications of the legislation, see Kent Roach, *September 11: Consequences for Canada* (Montreal: McGill-Queen's University Press, 2003). For a further discussion of the civil liberties implications of the legislation, see also David Schneiderman and Brenda Cossman, "Political Association and the Anti-Terrorism Bill," in Patrick Macklem and Kent Roach, *The Security of Freedom: Essays on Canada's Anti-Terrorism Bill* (Toronto: University of Toronto Press, 2001), p. 173–94; Tim Quigley, "New Anti-Terrorist Bills Could Criminalize Political Dissent," *CCPA Monitor* 9(10) April 2003, p. 1, 6–8. Ziyaad Mia, "Terrorizing the Rule of Law: Implications of the Anti-Terrorism Act," in Errol Mendes and Debar McAllister, (eds.), *National Journal of Constitutional Law* 14 (2002), p. 125–52; Don Stuart, "The Anti-Terrorism Bill C-36: An Unnecessary Law and Order Quick Fix that Permanently Stains the Canadian Criminal Justice System," in Errol Mendes and Debar McAllister, (eds.), *National Journal of Constitutional Law* 14 (2002), p. 153–68.

26. *Foreign Missions and International Organizations Act* SC 1991, c.41.

27. See Quigley, supra. note 24, p. 7.

28. *In the Shadow of Law: Report by the International Civil Liberties Monitoring Group*

in Response to Justice Canada's 1st Annual Report on the Application of the Anti-Terrorism Act (Bill C-36), insert, CAUT Bulletin, vol. 50, no. 6, 2003. The ICLMG membership includes: Amnesty International, Association québecoise des organaismes de cooperation internationale, Canadian Association of University Teachers, Canadian Arab Federation, Canadian Bar Association, Canadian Auto Workers Union, Canadian Centre for Philanthropy, Canadian Council for International Co-operation, Canadian Council for Refugees, Canadian Ethnocultural Council, Canadian Friends Service Committee, Canadian Labour Congress, CARE Canada, Centre for Social Justice, Council of Canadians, CUSO, B.C. Freedom of Information and Privacy Association, David Suzuki Foundation, Development and Peace, Greenpeace, International Development and Relief Foundation, Inter Pares, Muslim Lawyers Association, Ontario Council of Agencies Serving Immigrants, Primate's World Relief and Development Fund, Quebec Civil Liberties Union, Rights and Democracy, United Steelworkers of America, World Vision Canada.

29. Ibid.

30. See the collection of essays edited by Gary Kinsman, Dieter K. Buse and Mercedes Steedman, *Whose National Security? Canadian State Surveillance and the Creation of Enemies* (Toronto: Between the Lines Press, 2000).

31. There is a considerable literature on the SLAPP phenomenon. See George Pring and Penelope Canan, *SLAPPs: Getting Sued for Speaking Out* (Philadelphia: Temple University Press, 1996); J.E. Sills, "SLAPP: How Can the Legal System Eliminate Their Appeal?" *Connecticut Law Review* 25 (1993), p. 547–98; a relatively comprehensive bibliography on the subject is available from the California Anti-SLAPP Project at <www.casp.net/bibacad.html>.

32. See California Anti-SLAPP Project, *Survival Guide for SLAPP Victims,* available at <www.casp.net/survival.html>.

33. The causes of action presented below are available in most common law jurisdictions. They are described in very general terms and the exact details of what each cause of action involves may vary somewhat from jurisdiction to jurisdiction.

34. California Anti-SLAPP Project, <www.casp.net>.

35. *Protection of Public Participation Act,* SBC 2001, c.19.

36. Karen Wristen, Sierra Legal Defence Fund presentation given at the Western Mining Activist Network Conference, "Reaching into the Boardrooms," March 1999. Excerpt available at <www.miningwatch.org/emcbc/publications/toolkit/5.htm>. See also Virginia Rose Smith, "Canadians Ungagged: A Victory for Free Speech in *Daishowa Inc. v. Friends of the Lubicon,*" *Multinational Monitor* 19 (May 1998), p. 19–20, and Chris Tollefson, "Strategic Lawsuits and Environmental Politics: *Daishowa Inc. v. Friends of Lubicon,*" *Journal of Canadian Studies* 31 (1996), p. 119–33.

Chapter 4

The Politics of Rights

The assertion of rights has frequently been the vehicle by which legal activism has been pursued. Since World War II, rights and rights discourse have become an important part of the political culture of most western liberal democracies.[1] The concept of rights has become the lens through which individuals understand both their relationship to the state and to each other. In many respects we live in a society rooted in conceptions of rights. The specific nature of rights and the attachment people feel towards rights, however, vary from country to country. Americans hold to a vigorous understanding of individual rights, while the British have a much more limited commitment to rights.[2] These disparities can be explained by the country's particular history, along with the specific nature of its institutional and governmental structures. Given the importance of rights and rights discourse in civil society, however, it is not surprising that many groups seek to express their political aspirations through the language of rights.

There are advantages and disadvantages to pursuing a rights claim in the courts. On the one hand, rights can provide a powerful frame through which to articulate a political vision. The recognition and validation of a rights claim by the courts can be a significant accomplishment and can provide the basis for real political gains. Nevertheless, the constitutional articulation of rights is more limited than most people realize.

The Limits of Rights

While rights have become part of everyday discourse in western societies, their legal and institutional expression is usually through some form of constitutionally entrenched document. The *Canadian Charter of Rights and Freedoms*, the American *Bill of Rights* and the *European Convention on Human Rights* are all examples of documents that set out in legal terms the rights of citizens.[3] Although the exact formulation of these guarantees varies, most rights documents provide protection for the following general categories:

- democratic rights: right to vote, right to run for office, limits on the duration of legislatures;
- legal rights: the rights of those accused of criminal offences, including the right to a fair trial, the presumption of innocence, the right to a lawyer, the right to freedom from unreasonable search and seizure, etc.;
- fundamental freedoms: freedom of expression, freedom of religion, freedom of assembly and association; and
- equality rights: the right to equal treatment by the state and the right to freedom from discrimination. This is often accompanied by a list of potential prohibited grounds of discrimination such as race, religion, sex, age, mental or physical disability, sexual orientation and so on.

The constitutional expression of rights, however, is often very formalistic, and their interpretation by the courts frequently addresses neither the substantive causes of inequality nor the underlying power imbalances in society against which many social movements struggle. For this reason, rights, at least at the formal constitutional level, may prove relatively ineffective at promoting social change.

The limited nature of constitutional rights has much to do with their origins within liberal political thought. Classical liberal philosophers understood freedom and liberty in individualistic terms. Each individual possessed a sphere of personal autonomy that enabled that individual to pursue her own best (self) interests. This perspective led to an understanding of the state as a potential threat to freedom and to the insistence on a strict separation of the private and public realms. The state was accorded a limited public sphere in which it could legitimately act. Primarily, its role was to ensure that individuals had the fullest opportunity to enjoy their personal freedom. The state's role was a minimalist one, limited to such things as policing and national defence. It was considered illegitimate, however, for the state to intrude on the private realm of the individual. Matters of personal freedom, and most particularly, market relations and private property rights, were left to the individual, private sphere beyond the scope of state regulation. Matters of family life and religion were also considered part of the private realm. Rights, in this liberal conception, protect the private realm against state intrusions.

Legal structures in western democracies, then, are underpinned by the same principles of liberalism that inform the market economy and our democratic political institutions. Consequently, western jurisprudence is often described as reflecting a "legal liberalism" in which courts and law support the market economy, protect private property and reinforce an individualized conception of social relations. Rights are thought of as "trumps" that the individual has in her possession and which may be utilized against the state.[4]

Negative Rights

This approach leads to a conception of rights in liberal democracies that is both individualistic and negative. It is negative in that rights apply as a check on the activities of the state. Many people mistakenly view rights as protecting them both in their dealing with the state and with other people and institutions of society. Rights, however, usually only apply in contexts in which there is state action. Rights violations that occur within the realm of civil society, but without state action attached to them, are generally beyond the scope of most constitutional protections. Section 32 of the *Canadian Charter of Rights and Freedoms*, for example, makes this explicit, stating that, "this Charter applies to the Parliament and Government of Canada ... and ... to the legislatures and governments of each province."

A number of arguments have been made before the courts to extend the scope of the Charter to the private realm; most have been unsuccessful.[5] The American *Bill of Rights* also applies only to state action and does not extend into the realm of civil society. Inequality and discrimination that take place outside the scope of the state are largely beyond constitutional review. In other words, while the state cannot restrict freedom of expression, there is nothing to prevent a private employer from doing so, for example, by prohibiting electioneering at the workplace or by restricting workers' freedom of expression.

This is not to say that there is no

Is it Government?

The requirement that there be some "governmental" or state action before rights guarantees are applicable can lead to contradictory outcomes. Government employees, for example, may enjoy rights protections that are unavailable to private sector employees. If the government chooses to contract out certain functions, such as janitorial services, rights protections are suddenly lost.

In Canada, the courts have held that some broadly public institutions are sufficiently independent from government that the Charter does not apply to them. In *McKinney v. The University of Guelph* [1990] 3 *Supreme Court Reports* 229, a challenge to mandatory retirement provisions contained in a university collective agreement, the Supreme Court held that the university was sufficiently autonomous from government that the Charter did not apply. Community colleges, on the other hand, which are more directly regulated by government, have been found to be subject to the Charter. See *Lavigne v. Ontario Public Sector Employees Union* [1991] 2 *Supreme Court Reports* 211.

mechanism for redressing discrimination in the private realm. Pressure from social movements demanding equality have led to a number of legislative developments that seek to protect individual rights. Human rights codes throughout Canada, for example, prohibit discrimination on a range of grounds, including race, religion, age, sex, national or ethnic origin and disability. They apply to such private sector areas as housing, employment and the provision of services. In the United States, the *Civil Rights Act of 1964* attempted to address the lack of constitutional reach into the private realm. In the United Kingdom, the Commission for Racial Equality provides some protection against discrimination in the private realm, and specialized employment tribunals operate to provide redress where discrimination takes place in the workplace.

Although these non–constitutional mechanisms for addressing inequality are important, generally the range of protected rights are more limited than constitutionally entrenched rights. Human rights codes, for example, address discrimination but do not cover the full range of rights that would be included in a constitutionally entrenched bill of rights. Democratic rights, freedom of speech, assembly and association, as well as privacy and security rights, would not be included in most human rights codes. These rights, however, may be particularly important for social movement struggles. The public-private dichotomy, then, limits the potential utility of constitutional rights for social movement struggles.

Positive Rights

"Negative" and "individual" rights can be usefully contrasted with "positive" and "collective" rights. As discussed above, negative rights place limits on the state and prevent it from acting in particular ways. A positive right, on the other hand, imposes obligations on the state, requiring it to ensure that individuals or groups are able to exercise their rights. Negative rights clearly derive from the liberal tradition and predominate in most constitutional orders. The American *Bill of Rights*, for example, explicitly favours a negative rights formulation. The framers of the American constitution, reacting to what they saw as the excesses of the British imperial government, defined rights not in terms of the citizen, but rather as express limits on the state. The *First Amendment*, for example, articulates fundamental freedoms such as freedom of religion and speech as prohibitions on Congress's legislative power. Critics of rights-based politics argue that the negative focus of most constitutional protections unnecessarily casts the state as the enemy of liberty, and consequently ignores the potential of the state to redress social inequality and social injustice.[6]

For a social action group seeking to push the state to redress a social inequity, positive rights will often be of greater utility than negative rights. Section 7 of the *Canadian Charter of Rights and Freedoms*, for example, provides that everyone has the "right to life, liberty, and security of the person, and the right not to be deprived thereof except in accordance with the principles of fundamental justice." This is potentially a very broad right. How broad, however, depends in part on whether it is conceptualized in negative or positive terms. A negative rights interpretation would simply preclude state actions depriving individuals of their life, liberty or security of their person. Illegal incarceration, for example, would clearly be prohibited, as would things such as torture, forced sterilization and perhaps even state seizure of property without compensation. In each of these cases, however, we deal with a prohibition on state activity that in some way infringes on individual liberty and freedom.

An approach that emphasizes positive rights, however, produces very different outcomes. For example, secu-

Positive Rights v. Negative Rights

The case of *Eldridge v. British Columbia* [1997] 3 *Supreme Court Reports* 624 provides a good example of a positive rights approach in judicial decision-making. Sign language interpretation for the hearing impaired in British Columbia hospitals had been provided by a private non-profit organization, which had received no government support. Because of financial constraints, the organization applied for funding from the government, which refused to grant it any resources. As a result, it was forced to terminate its sign language services. The lawsuit argued that the actions of the government had violated the equality rights of those with hearing disabilities. The government responded with a "negative rights" argument. Health care, it argued, was available equally to all and there was no discrimination in access. The provision of sign language translation had not been a government service and the government had not engaged in any direct action itself that had discriminated against the hearing impaired. The court rejected this argument, holding that the failure to provide funding for sign language interpretation resulted in differential levels of service and that the government was required to take positive steps to ensure that those with hearing disabilities received a comparable level of service, not just the same right of access.

rity of the person, when viewed from a positive perspective, might include state obligations to ensure adequate housing and health care, or minimum standards of education and income. Social activists might utilize a positive rights interpretation to compel the state to implement measures designed to ensure the security of the person. It would provide a powerful lever to question the substantive conditions of social existence and to make arguments about the nature of state obligations to rectify inequality. In effect, then, the difference between negative and positive rights is analogous to the difference between the liberal conception of equal opportunity, which is formalistic and procedural, and more communitarian or socialist visions of equality, which seek to examine the actual social conditions necessary to achieve substantive equality.

Perhaps it is not surprising that the courts have been reluctant to accept an interpretation of rights that would impose obligations on the state. To do so would involve the courts much more explicitly in the political task of judging substantive policies enacted by governments. The legitimacy of the courts depends on maintaining the distinction between law and politics. Politicians, who are accountable to the people through elections, are generally viewed as responsible for developing and implementing public policy. Courts, it is argued, should stick to the law.[7] In other words, while judges may occasionally be called upon to interpret laws and even to judge the constitutional legality of laws, they are not involved in the political task of adjudicating the substantive merits and wisdom of particular legislative choices. Moreover, it is considered beyond the legitimate mandate of judges to, in effect, prescribe to the legislature what should be included in the law.

Of course, the distinction between law and politics is, to a certain extent, a fiction. In making their decisions, judges frequently bring to bear ideological presuppositions and a political viewpoint. Indeed, the very choice of interpreting rights as a negative constraint on state power is an ideological and political one. Nonetheless, it is easier to justify intervening and overturning state policy when the rationale for doing so is cast in a negative rights framework. It is far more difficult, for example, to justify the courts dictating to the legislature what is necessary for a "constitution-ally acceptable" health care program. This means, however, that even when a social action group is successful before the courts, it is unlikely the courts will provide a remedy that achieves the goals and objectives of the group. Rather, the court is far more likely to declare a law invalid and leave it up to the legislature to determine how to rectify the constitutional deficiency. In some cases the court may even suspend the declaration of invalidity to give the government an opportunity to design new legisla-tion.

There are instances where courts may be more willing to compel the government to take positive action. In particular, this may occur in equality cases where the problem stems from the "under-inclusive" nature of legislation. This sort of situation emerges when the state extends a benefit to some members of society but not to others. The difficulty is not with the legislation per se. There is nothing inherently offensive or unconstitutional about the nature of the benefit. Rather, the problem rests with the fact that certain groups are not included within the scope of the benefit. There are a number of such examples: differential parental leaves for biological and adoptive parents,[8] pension benefits available to hetero-sexual couples but not to same-sex couples,[9] or translation services made available to some communities but not to others.[10] In these instances, should the court simply declare the law invalid, not only would those seeking a remedy not benefit but those currently enjoying the program would also lose out. In some instances the courts may choose to "read into" the statute the excluded group. This rests on the assumption that the legislature unintentionally passed an unconstitutional law and therefore it is acceptable for the court to "add in" the excluded group to preserve the constitutional integrity of the legislation.[11]

While the courts may now occasionally dictate to the government what it should do to meet the requirements of the constitution, they are generally very reluctant to engage in this practice. It is far more common for the courts to simply issue a declaration of invalidity, but suspend its operation while the government makes amendments to bring the program in question into line with the requirements of the constitution. It is critical to remember, however, that the range of options available to the government may be fairly wide. It could choose to allocate new money to a program to accommodate the inclusion of previously excluded groups. Another option would be to extend the scope of a program but retain funding at current levels, with the result that benefits to everyone are reduced. It is even conceivable that the government could simply repeal a program completely. Eliminating a program would likely carry with it very negative political consequences, particularly if it is a popular one. A number of governments have found it difficult to significantly narrow the scope of the welfare state, particularly in core areas such as health care and education. Nevertheless, since rights are generally under-stood as limits on the state, rather than obligations, this possibility still exists.

This is not to say that courts do not occasionally impose obligations on the state. The concepts of negative and positive rights are ideal types, and frequently the application of rights in specific situations may display elements of both. Nevertheless, where the courts display a more positive rights orientation, it tends to be somewhat hesitant and limited in scope. Rarely would a social action group find the court imposing broad positive obligations on the state. The prevalence of a negative rights framework highlights the need to consider rights cases within the context of a broader political struggle. Victory in court rarely results in achievement of a group's goals, and it will generally be necessary to continue pressuring the state through other political channels.

Collective Rights

Rights are also conceptualized in individualistic terms, almost as a form of property. Of course, this perspective is perfectly consistent with liberalism's overwhelming preoccupation with the individual. Collective or group rights, on the other hand, are relatively rare in most constitutional documents. Individuals enjoy such rights not because of their status as individuals, but rather because of their membership in a particular collectivity. The Canadian constitution, while largely an individual rights document, does contain some important collective rights. Aboriginal rights, which are protected in section 25 of the Charter and section 35 of the Canadian constitution, are important examples of collective rights enjoyed by a particular minority community.[12] Similarly, the constitution also provides some protection for minority language education rights.[13]

Generally, however, examples of such collective rights are rare. The preference of the courts for an individualistic approach can adversely affect rights claims advanced by social action groups. This has certainly been the experience of the labour movement, which attempted to rely on the Charter to safeguard collective bargaining and the right to strike against legislative erosion. During the 1980s, the federal government and a number of provincial governments introduced legislation restricting collective bargaining rights and the right to strike for public sector workers.[14]

Public sector labour unions responded by arguing before the courts that this legislation violated the guarantee of freedom of association found in section 2(d) of the Charter. In a series of cases known as the "labour trilogy," the unions advanced what was essentially a collectivist understanding of associational rights.[15] They argued that trade unions are a particular sort of association with very specific objectives and purposes, namely the collective representation of workers. Collective bargaining and the capacity to withdraw labour power are critical to this purpose. Legislative curtailment of these facets of union activity, they argued, undermined the right to join a union by undermining the very rationale for the union's existence. In other words, the union as a collectivity possessed certain rights as a result of the associational interests of its individual members.

The courts rejected this argument, interpreting association as an individual right. In other words, Charter protection bestowed on individuals the right to become members of a group or organization, but nothing beyond this. The activities of the group gained no special constitutional protection and could be subject to legislative curtailment, unless they could be performed individually and were subject to some other constitutional protection (such as freedom of expression). State restrictions on the collective bargaining or the right to strike did not, in the court's view, affect the individual's capacity to join a union, nor were these activities otherwise protected by the constitution. Consequently, there was no violation of the Charter. Such an approach considers association from an individualist perspective, removing the individual from her collective existence. As a result, the labour movement was left with little faith in the *Canadian Charter of Rights and Freedoms* to help stem the tide of neo-liberal, anti-union measures that dominated the 1980s and 1990s. Indeed, after the "labour trilogy," the labour movement generally abandoned attempts to use the courts to advance political goals.

The Potential of Rights

The criticisms above clearly demonstrate the congruence of judicial interpretations of rights and the fundamental principles of classic liberalism. It is this congruence that has led many commentators to describe the attitude of judges and lawyers, as well as the core principles of rights jurisprudence, as reflecting a legal liberalism. Nevertheless, despite the limits of legal liberalism, rights claims may, in some circumstances, be extremely useful to a social action group's political strategy. The constraints and limits of rights are very real; however, they do not necessarily preclude utilizing rights and courts as part of a political struggle. The significance of these limits can be overestimated by adopting a framework in which winning or losing a case before the courts is the critical element of the struggle. Rather, it is important to not conceptualize "the case" in a vacuum but understand it in terms of its relationship to the broader struggle.

This is precisely what Michael McCann and Helena Silverstein attempted to do in developing a "legal mobilization framework." For McCann and Silverstein, legal norms, principles and practices provide:

> some of the most important strategies of action that citizens routinely mobilize to negotiate relations, whether cooperative or conflictual, with each other and the state. Hence, the most

distinctive contribution of the legal mobilization approach—that of shifting the focus of legal analysis away from the initiative of judges and state officials towards that of politically active citizens, and away from "law on the books" to law as a resource in practical political struggle.[16]

Thinking of law in these terms allows us to move beyond rigid dichotomies and the idea of the judicial outcome as a "zero-sum" game of winning and losing. Indeed, it permits us to begin developing a more contextualized understanding of the benefits that rights claims (as well as other forms of legal claims) might offer to a social action group.

One potential benefit of rights-based action is that it may serve as a powerful catalyst. The language of rights highlights injustices as well as expresses the determination/need for a remedy. In this context, it is precisely the liberal understanding of a right as something possessed by an individual that makes this claim so powerful. Rights consolidate and render concrete the injustices and grievances people experience, while legitimizing the demand for change. The assertion of rights can play a role in "elevating citizen expectations, generating new claims of entitlement, and expanding options for realistic change. These contributions to consciousness-raising in turn can activate constituent support and catalyze movement building."[17]

Of course, developing a litigation strategy does not necessarily lead to mobilization. One of the criticisms of so-called "legalized politics" is its potential for demobilization. Whether the pursuit of a claim contributes to the development of the social action group will depend on a number of factors. These include the nature of rights claim advanced, the group's capacity to develop an effective frame for its issues, the group's organizational structure and the nature of the movement's constituency.

Litigation, on its own, rarely provides the basis for organizing and mobilizing a movement. Where a group has already formed or is in the process of mobilizing, litigation can crystallize the movement and aid in the recruitment and retention of members. The early legal victories of the American civil rights movement in cases like *Brown v. The Board of Education*[18] helped mobilize grassroots African-Americans against segregation and played an important part in the eventual passage of the *Civil Rights Act* by the U.S. federal government. As McCann and Silverstein state:

Such cases raised the expectations of southern blacks, sparked grassroots activism, and encouraged movement organization on multiple fronts. It is true that court decisions mobilized a reactionary counter-movement among southern whites, of course, but this only prompted federal officials to back up the courts with coercive power and to support the growing grassroots activism for equal rights. In these ways, legal action virtually catalyzed a movement that eventually transcended legal tactics altogether in its goal of advancing basic democratic goals.[19]

It is far too easy to dismiss the significance of these cases on the basis that they did not bring an end to inequality and discrimination, but few would argue that this could be accomplished by a single judicial decision. Those early civil rights victories were significant moments in the formation of a movement; they offered hope and inspiration, shed light on the degree to which racism was inscribed in American institutions and mobilized people against segregation. Other groups, including the women's movement,[20] the pro-choice movement,[21] the mental health movement,[22] anti-racist groups,[23] the gay and lesbian movement,[24] and environmental movements[25] have all made strategic use of litigation, but with varying degrees of success.

It is one thing to mobilize around a victory, but what about a defeat? How important are victories to the utilization of rights claims by social movements? Victory has been the subject of much discussion by sceptics of rights-based claims. Some analysts point to the fact that social movements lose more often than they win, and even when they do win, the victory does not always bring the desired social change. From this perspective, going to court, engaging in a legal battle that may take years and spending considerable group resources may not appear to be a wise decision. This criticism, however, once again relies on an all-or-nothing understanding of legal activism. Victories and defeats may both support and encourage mobilization, or impede and limit successful mobilization. Much depends on how the group's leadership strategically organizes itself around the litigation.

A victory, for example, may lead the group to be complacent and to stop or limit its mobilization efforts. In part, this may depend on the nature of the victory. Political demobilization is unlikely to occur in a multi-dimensional campaign. Winning a desegregation fight in a single school, for example, does not automatically lead to desegregation in other contexts. This is because the "reach" of any particular judicial decision generally doesn't go beyond the facts of the specific case. Consequently, a victory of this sort advances civil rights but points to other areas that remain unaddressed. Bus service, employment opportunities, housing and a host of other issues might still need to be addressed, perhaps through litigation but potentially through other political means.

In a single issue campaign, however, the situation may be quite the opposite. Here, the potential for demobilization is greater. The U.S. Supreme Court decision in *Roe v. Wade*,[26] which affirmed women's rights to abortion, has been blamed for displacing this issue from the political arena into the judicial realm. To some extent the decision gave pro-choice groups in the United States a false sense of security and left them ill-prepared to respond to the conservative assault on abortion rights. During the last American presidential election campaign, discussions of the implications of a Bush victory frequently centred on appointments to the American Supreme Court and the likely reversal of the *Roe* decision. In situations like this, victory on the specific case is precisely what is being sought. Consequently, the need for further mobilization may not be readily apparent.[27]

The degree to which a rights case leads to mobilization also depends on the nature of the specific claim. To be successful, a rights claim needs to be translated into a broad appeal that motivates people to become involved in the group's struggle. Generally, there is a narrowing of issues as a dispute becomes embedded within a formal legal procedure. However, disputes may also be expanded and reshaped in a framework not necessarily accepted by either the formal decision-maker or the other parties to the dispute.[28] Cases that raise broad issues of justice and equality can be more easily reshaped in this fashion than cases that raise narrow technical issues.

For this reason, rights cases are generally better suited to a mobilization campaign than other sorts of legal claims, such as civil suits or administrative law cases, which tend to raise narrow and highly technical issues. The flexibility of rights language is particularly useful in this regard. Even though a rights issue may, in the courts, be understood in a fairly limited and technical way, it can easily be integrated into material for public consumption that utilizes a broader and less legalistic interpretation of rights. The social action group can successfully translate rights issues into a non-legal format that resonates with its membership and with the broader community.

An example of this sort of "translation" is reflected in the recent debates on the Canadian government's attempts to establish a firearms registry. As a justification for disobeying the *Firearms Registration Act*, Ed

Hudson, Secretary of the Canadian Unregistered Firearm Owners Association, invoked the *Canadian Charter of Rights and Freedoms.*[29] In particular, he argued in unequivocal terms that the legislation violated seven different rights guaranteed by the Charter. These included the rights to "privacy, mobility, security from unreasonable search and seizure, presumption of innocence, representation, freedom of association and against self-incrimination." He concluded that "fair-minded judges" would never uphold the law and that the legislation is so unreasonable and unfair that civil disobedience would be justified.

No legal argument is advanced for just how the *Firearms Registration Act* violates the Charter, and indeed, one would be hard pressed to argue in favour of Hudson's claims in the courts. Nevertheless, for the purpose of mobilization this is irrelevant. Hudson has successfully made a rights-based claim —through the media rather than through the courts—which will resonate with opponents of gun control. It does not matter, for example, that the Charter contains no explicit right to privacy, or that the *Firearms Registration Act* contains nothing to prevent one from having legal representation or forces one to testify against oneself (self-incrimination). Should any future litigation regarding the constitutionality of the legislation be lost, as is likely to be the case, Hudson already has his answer ready. "Fair-minded judges" would not come to such a conclusion. The judiciary itself has somehow been corrupted, thereby further justifying the movement's orientation towards civil disobedience.[30]

This example is useful because it demonstrates how a rights discourse, from a movement's perspective, does not depend on strict legal interpretation. Indeed, legal interpretation may simply bog down a group's appeal to justice with needless details and technicalities. Other than lawyers and the individual accused, who is really interested in the details of self-incrimination law? The example also demonstrates that rights claims are not just made by equity-seeking movements, but also by movements on the right of the political spectrum. Indeed, rights claims may actually be of greater benefit to right-wing social action groups because of the basic ideological congruence of their belief in individualism with the ideological underpinnings of law and rights.

However, it is also possible for equity seeking and social justice movements, such as anti-poverty activists, housing advocates, environmentalists, women's groups and others, to also recast and reshape rights claims for public consumption as a way of engaging in movement building. Anti-poverty activists, for example, have used the discourse of rights to assert claims to better and improved social services. In this context welfare benefits that provide an adequate standard of living are viewed as a right of citizenship. The women's movement has used rights as the basis for claiming reproductive freedom and access to abortion services and for insisting on such diverse public policies as employment equity, transition houses for battered women, and women's health clinics.

It is possible to make such rights claims without going to court. However, advancing these arguments in the judicial arena can carry some important strategic benefits. For one thing, going to court can give the group a focus and a purpose. There is a great deal of work to be done to successfully pursue a court case. Contrary to the impression left by critics of rights politics, the case is not conducted exclusively by lawyers. Group members raise funds for the court case, conduct public meetings to inform people about the case, develop brochures, pamphlets and other public education materials and hold news conferences. Actions can be planned and coordinated with the bringing of the litigation. Mock trials of the case can be held in the lead-up to the actual hearing. Demonstrations outside the legislature and the courthouse when the matter is being heard can help mobilize members of the group. In this regard, the group needs to think of the court case as a focal point for a diversity of action, rather than as a substitute for action.

Taking a rights case to court may also bring considerable public and media attention. The media gives human rights cases a relatively high profile. Bringing a case to court, therefore, may give a group and its issues attention that it might otherwise not achieve. This is particularly so if the case is accompanied by other political action. Regardless of whether the case produces a victory, judicial action provides a vehicle by which the group's message and issues can reach a wider audience.

Dealing with the media, however, is always somewhat problematic. The group's message may be inaccurately or incompletely presented. This is always a danger for groups dealing with the mainstream media, but the problem is exacerbated with court cases. Press coverage of legal issues is frequently very poor and demonstrates a lack of understanding of law and judicial issues. As such, group representatives need to be well-schooled in the relevant legal issues and be able to relate them to the group's broader political concerns.

Many groups rely on their lawyers to deal with the media. Although this may be a good strategy, it does have its limitations. First, a lawyer may focus on the legal issue before the court and be reticent to comment on its political ramifications or on the group's political agenda. Lawyers may be criticized by judges for "arguing the case in the press" rather than confining their submissions to the courtroom. During the Supreme Court of Canada hearings in the *Operation Dismantle* case, for example, Chief Justice Bora Laskin chastised Operation Dismantle's lawyer, Lawrence Greenspon, for arguing the merits of his position before the press.[31] The degree to which lawyers feel comfortable advocating the "political message" of the group before the press will depend, in part, on the political and legal culture that prevails. In the United States there is a much greater tendency for lawyers to court public opinion by playing to the media. In Canada and the United Kingdom, on the other hand, where greater restrictions on press coverage of court cases have always existed, lawyers are much more circumspect. In these situations, therefore, it may be preferable to have a well-versed spokesperson represent the public face of the group. This requires group members to educate themselves about the legal issues and not simply turn the case over to the lawyers.

Another advantage of actually commencing a lawsuit is that it may permit the group to become involved in policy debates with governmental decision-makers. Litigation generally does not proceed directly from the issuing of a claim to the trial of the matter in court. There is often opportunity for the parties to negotiate and discuss potential settlements. Where a matter of public policy is at stake, as is frequently the situation in human rights cases, the litigation provides the group with an opportunity to consult decision-makers and potentially affect policy outcomes. McCann and Silverstein refer to this aspect of a litigation strategy as "leveraging access."[32]

Such access may be used to influence the development of policy, but also to alter the manner by which it is implemented. This approach may certainly be used in human rights cases, but also in a wide range of other sorts of cases. Although the primary concern may be with gaining access to the state, it may also serve as a vehicle by which private corporations are forced to sit down and talk with social action groups concerned about the public impact of their activities. The experience of SLAPPs discussed in Chapter 3, however, suggests that corporations, in particular, may prefer to fight rather than talk.

Employing litigation to gain access to the state rests on several interrelated assumptions about the nature of law and state policy processes. First, it is important to realize that pursuing litigation as a leveraging strategy shifts the objectives of the group. The concern is not necessarily with winning or losing the case, but rather with the sort of access that can be gained from the strategy. Litigation becomes a pressure tactic to force the state (or other opponents) into making concessions. In this context, it may not even be necessary to pursue the litigation through to completion. Winning the case becomes less important than securing legislative or regulatory changes from the state. This underscores the artificiality of the distinction made by many critics of rights-based politics between legislative and judicial arenas.

Second, it is important to remember that litigation has financial implications not only for the group but also for the state. These costs include staff time, both for government lawyers and for other employees who may be involved in preparing the case, gathering documents and testifying before the courts. Where the case involves specialized knowledge or expertise, there may be a need for expert witnesses. The litigation may also delay the implementation of a program or policy, thereby increasing its implementation costs. The costs to the state, therefore, are significant. Moreover these costs can be even higher if the state decides to hire non-government lawyers to argue the case before the courts of appeal. In addition, going to court carries the risk of the state losing control of its own policy process. The court's final decision may require policy changes that are more expensive or (from the government's perspective) less desirable than other alternatives that all parties might have agreed to as a settlement of the case. There may be, therefore, ample reason for the government to consider negotiating a settlement that keeps the case out of court.

Finally, this approach rests on the assumption that the courts are not the only institution capable of discussing, adjudicating and coming to conclusions about the merits of rights claims.[33] Constitutionally, the courts have a special and privileged role in this regard. They are the final arbiters on the meaning of constitutionally protected rights (they also have the final say on interpreting any statute or regulation). However, legislators and bureaucrats also discuss the meaning of rights and the implications of different policy options for members of the public. Indeed, the existence of constitutionally protected rights requires that state actors other than judges involve themselves in these sorts of discussions.[34]

Section 1 of the *Canadian Charter of Rights and Freedoms* illustrates this point. It provides that:

> The rights contained herein are subject to such reasonable limits, prescribed by law, as can be demonstrably justified in a free and democratic society.

The Canadian courts have interpreted this section as requiring a "balancing" of the objectives of legislation against the severity of the rights violation. This balancing process requires that governments generally choose the method of achieving their policy goals that least intrudes on people's rights.[35] It would be a highly imprudent government that pursued a policy with negative rights implications without having engaged in this assessment itself. Policymakers want/need to know whether their policies could violate constitutional guarantees, what possibilities exist for withstanding a constitutional challenge and what likelihood there is that a challenge will be brought. Designing policy in a way that minimizes the risk of judicial scrutiny has necessarily become part of the policy process.[36] Social action groups can use the threat of litigation to insert themselves into these discussions. This may raise issues and provide a context to the discussions that might otherwise not be considered within the bureaucracy.

Like any strategy of pressuring the state, a number of factors will affect the likelihood of success. One important factor is the existence of supportive case law. The degree to which a litigation strategy can be used will depend in part on its potential for success. The greater the chance of success, the more willing the state will be to avoid the costs of litigation and a potentially embarrassing defeat. This does not mean the case must be a sure win for the social movement. Rather, the case law must be sufficiently supportive of the movement's position for a reasonable chance of victory. If the case law is completely unsupportive, the state may be more willing to stick to its position and seek judicial vindication. A victory in the courts does offer the state enhanced legitimacy for a policy that might otherwise be viewed as suspect.

From the group's perspective, this requires a delicate assessment of the chances for litigation success. It is rare, however, that success can be predicted with absolute certainty. Rather, outcomes are often uncertain and depend on the judge hearing the case, the nature of the evidence presented, the existence of supporting and detracting judicial precedents and the skills of the lawyers involved. Most lawyers are reluctant (and rightly so) to give odds on the chances for success. Generally, the best one can expect is a "good" or "reasonable" chance of success.

Even if the objective of launching a case is to leverage access to the state rather than pursue the litigation to its final conclusion, the group must be prepared for this possibility. If the state refuses to negotiate, or if discussions fail to produce satisfactory policy outcomes, the group may feel it has no other alternative but to proceed with the litigation. Since the group must be prepared to go all the way if necessary, it should try to ensure that it has the necessary organizational structure and resources (money) to support the case. If the opposition feels the group is lacking in resources, it may pursue the litigation rather than negotiate, in the hope that the group will be unable to sustain the litigation and be forced to drop the case.

Certain types of groups may be better suited to pursuing litigation as a political strategy than others. Larger, more institutionalized groups, or those with a mass membership that can be relied on for financial support, will generally have a better chance of weathering the financial storm of a lawsuit. Small, grassroots organizations will have a much harder time carrying litigation through to completion on their own. This does not, however, necessarily preclude this strategy, even for small groups. Litigation may represent an opportunity to bring into the group more members and more resources. It may also provide an opportunity to form coalitions and alliances with other, better-funded social movement organizations. The group can enhance its resources and establish potentially important alliances by creating a network of groups with a shared concern. A local struggle can potentially generate national alliances and draw national attention in this fashion.

The success of litigation as a mechanism for gaining access to the decision-making process may also depend on how far advanced the policy process is at the time. The state may be more receptive to negotiating with a group early in the policy process, prior to firm decisions being made, rather than in its later stages when policy positions have crystallized. In other words, litigation may provide a more useful tool for securing a place at the table rather than for changing the outcome of the decisions made at that table. At the latter point, the government's position as well as the positions of those who stand to benefit from it will be more firmly entrenched and the costs of altering the decision will be more significant. There is, therefore, a greater possibility that the government will take a hard line against litigation designed to alter policies at the implementation stage. By doing otherwise, the government risks appearing weak and indecisive, and increases the likelihood of angering those other organized parties who thought they had an "understanding" with the government as to the future direction of its policies.

Here the question of judicial support becomes important once again. Generally speaking courts have been less willing to oversee how policies are implemented. In the face of judicial reticence, governments may feel they are on fairly safe ground if they refuse to negotiate with groups dissatisfied with how a policy is implemented. For the courts, it is one thing to state that a government action is unconstitutional but quite another to supervise how policies are implemented to ensure their compliance with constitutional standards. The latter involves the court in a far more political and administrative process and, consequently, challenges the separation of law and politics upon which the court's legitimacy rests. Moreover, the courts tend to lack the resources to engage in this sort of activity:[37] judges lack the expertise and staff needed to analyze complex policy issues, and the adversarial process, which is party driven, does not offer the court a proactive and ongoing role in overseeing policy implementation. Instead, the courts must wait for dissatisfied and aggrieved persons to bring a case before them. Finally, the courts also tend to lack the capacity (or are unwilling) to direct the state as to how it should spend public monies.

Of course, the degree to which courts wish to be involved in implementation debates varies from jurisdiction to jurisdiction. Canada and Britain, for example, have far more conservative judicial traditions than the United States. To a great extent this reflects the absence of a human rights tradition in the United Kingdom and its relative youth in Canada.[38] As discussed above, Canadian courts have become more willing to order the state to take proactive measures in equality cases; however, they leave the mechanism for implementing those measures to the discretion of the government. Nevertheless, the recent decision of the Canadian Supreme Court in the case of *Doucet-Boudreau v. Nova Scotia (Minister of Education)* may signal a growing willingness to engage in judicial supervision where governments appear unwilling to meet the requirements of the Charter.[39] The court, by a narrow majority, endorsed a lower court's decision to order the Nova Scotia government to establish French language educational facilities and to schedule future hearings to monitor the government's progress.

This contrasts with the relatively richer tradition of American courts, which have frequently become involved in the workings of social institutions where constitutional issues of equality and discrimination are present. One of the best examples is the judicial involvement in civil rights, particularly around the issues of public school desegregation and school busing.

Initial decisions of the U.S. Supreme Court declaring the formal segregation of schools unconstitutional failed to address de facto segregation that resulted from the out-migration of white families to the suburbs. The courts subsequently ruled that African-American students from city centres would be bused to suburban schools to achieve the goal of racial integration. This resulted in protracted litigation before the courts overseeing the administration and adequacy of busing programs. In the end, the programs were widely viewed as a failure and the American experience has become a cautionary tale of the courts' inability to engage effectively in implementation debates.[40]

Certainly the American experience of judicial activism was not without its costs. Increased judicial intervention in a range of institutions generated a political backlash that enabled the neo-conservative governments of Reagan and Bush to reverse many of the advances in social justice that had been achieved with judicial support. This is particularly true in the areas of equality law, where employment equity was legislatively eroded, and reproductive freedom, where the legacy of *Roe v. Wade* has been greatly undermined. It also led to the replacement of retiring Supreme Court judges with extremely conservative judges hostile to progressive causes. American courts, therefore, are currently far less supportive of social action groups than they once were.[41]

The reticence of the courts to engage in debates about how policies should be implemented does not, however, mean that law has no role to play in this area. The growth of the welfare state was accompanied by a tremendous increase in the number of administrative and regulatory bodies that employ court-like processes. These quasi-judicial bodies, such as labour boards and environmental assessment boards, often shape the implementation of policy to a far greater degree than do politicians. Indeed, as will be discussed in Chapter 6, administrative bodies of this sort were created specifically to remove issues from the political realm and give a judicial air to the administration of potentially contentious policy areas. In these situations, engaging with the policy process almost necessarily involves engaging with these quasi-judicial bodies.

Rights, Courts and the Legitimacy of Coercion

So far, the book has focused primarily on situations in which a social action group chooses to utilize the courts to advance a rights claim. It is important to keep in mind, however, that going to court may not be so much a choice as a necessity. In many instances groups may seek recourse to the courts because they have exhausted all other avenues for advancing their claims. When lobbying, demonstrating, petitioning and other mechanisms for pressuring legislative and bureaucratic officials fail to produce substantive change, a group may feel it has little option but to pursue the issue in the courts. Going to court may be a last-ditch effort to block a state policy after all other avenues of opposition have failed.

Critics of rights politics argue that utilizing rights and law casts the state as an enemy rather than a vehicle by which progressive change can be accomplished. Casting the state as the enemy, so the argument goes, plays into the hands of the right, which then attacks the state as a threat to liberty and freedom of the market.[42] This approach reflects a social democratic perspective in which the state is the mechanism for redistributing wealth and remedying social problems. Undoubtedly, the state can and should be this mechanism. However, it is important to keep in mind that in very few places is the state as beneficent as the critique of rights politics would suggest.

One defining characteristic of the state is its monopoly over the legitimate use of coercive power in society. While such a definition may be incomplete, it certainly strikes at a core element of state power. The state does possess tremendous resources that may be used to coerce and discipline (repress) its citizens and residents. Many scholars have focused on the state's capacity to maintain its legitimacy through liberal ideology and the rule of law. Nevertheless, it is important to remember that the capacity to exercise coercion underpins state authority. In this sense, rights and courts play a highly contradictory role. Courts and conceptions of rights legitimize state rule and are also vehicles by which coercion (particularly by the police) is regularized and structured. They are both ideological and coercive state apparatuses that serve to authorize and legitimize the state's use of force. For this reason, however, courts are also arenas in which the use of force and repression can be held up for scrutiny and criticism.

As shown in Chapter 3, the exercise of dissent is increasingly subject to restriction and constraint. However, courts and rights can be used by those who have been arrested and incarcerated for engaging in dissent to challenge these measures. Conceptions of freedom of expression and freedom of association become important resources for challenging state measures that target and repress those who disagree with current political priorities.

There are many examples of individuals and groups engaging in the legal realm not out of choice but because they were arrested and brought before the courts. This includes those who have been arrested in protests and demonstrations. It also includes those who have had benefits taken away or been deprived of services. Anti-globalization activists arrested by the police during a demonstration, Aboriginal people arrested during a blockade of a logging road or for hunting and fishing without a licence, welfare claimants appealing termination of their benefits, squatters evicted and arrested or detained for trespassing: all are examples of those who have confronted the law. In these cases, going to court is necessary to win back a benefit or to ensure that demonstrations and protests may continue in the future.

It is true, of course, that in some of these cases, the groups and individuals involved deliberately seek conflict with authorities. Peaceful civil disobedience has long been a mechanism by which the injustice of particular laws can be highlighted. Aboriginal groups in Canada, for example, have deliberately violated hunting and fishing regulations to advance claims before the courts that their traditional land use practices require protection under the constitution. Similarly, the Canadian Abortion Rights Action League deliberately invited Dr. Henry Morgentaler to set up an abortion clinic in Toronto with the hope that he would be charged with violating the *Criminal Code* provisions prohibiting abortion. Morgentaler accepted the invitation, was charged, and the case eventually went to the Supreme Court of Canada and resulted in the abortion law being declared unconstitutional.[43]

In all of these cases, however, confronting the authorities necessarily involved breaking the law and inviting prosecution. The state, in both the Aboriginal land use and the abortion rights contexts, had proved either intransigent or unwilling to move with expediency. In this regard, it is important to remember that the state is not always beneficent. Indeed, governments in the western world have been dominated by neo-liberal and neo-conservative regimes since the mid-1970s, driven by the goal of reducing government services in favour of market solutions to social problems. In this context, the state may very well be the enemy of social movements, undoing many of the progressive changes brought about through their political pressure. Moreover, in recent years the assault on social movements and social programs has been more vigorously pursued by governments in the west. This is certainly true in the United States under George W. Bush and in Canada under the conservative provincial governments of Mike Harris, Ralph Klein and Gordon Campbell. It has also been true under the Labour government of Tony Blair in the United Kingdom.[44] Given this, one should not put too much faith in the state as a force for progressive change. To achieve such a result, we would need a very different state from those that currently exist. Law, rights and courts may, therefore, be important tools for resisting some of the attacks on the disenfranchised members of society.

Notes

1. See Alan Cairns, *Charter versus Federalism: The Dilemmas of Constitutional Reform* (Montreal, Kingston: McGill-Queen's University Press, 1992), ch. 1. See also Maxwell Cohen, "Human Rights: Programme or Catchall? A Canadian Rationale," *Canadian Bar Review* 46 (1968), p. 554.
2. For a discussion of the pre-eminence of individual rights in the American context, see Charles Epp, *The Rights Revolution: Lawyers, Activists, and Supreme Courts in Comparative Perspective* (Chicago: University of Chicago Press, 1998). For a discussion of rights in the British constitution, see Murray Hunt, *Using Human Rights Law in English Courts* (Oxford: Hart Publishing, 1997). See also Byron Sheldrick, "Judicial Review and Judicial Reticence: The Protection of Political Expression under the Common Law," *Journal of Civil Liberties* 3 (1998), p. 191–206.
3. It is important to note that not all constitutionally protected rights have the same scope of applicability. Some rights may only apply to actual citizens of a country, while others may apply to any person resident in the country. Careful attention must be paid to the written formulation of the rights and any limitations contained therein.
4. Ronald Dworkin, *Taking Rights Seriously* (Cambridge: Harvard University Press, 1977).
5. See Dale Gibson, "The Charter of Rights and the Private Sector," *Manitoba Law Journal* 12 (1982), p. 218, for an argument that the Charter does apply to the private realm. See also John Whyte, "Is the Private Sector Affected by the Charter?" in Lynn Smith (ed.), *Righting the Balance: Canada's New Equality Rights* (Saskatoon: Canadian Human Rights Reporter, 1986), p. 145, in which Whyte concludes that the framers of the Charter opted for the position that "in our role as private persons we are not obliged to subscribe to, and lead our lives according to, 'state' virtues" (at p. 149). In *Retail, Wholesale and Department Store Union, Local 580 v. Dolphin Delivery Ltd.* [1986] 2 S.C.R 573, the Supreme Court declined to apply the Charter to private litigation.
6. See, for example, Allen Hutchinson and Andrew Petter, "Private Rights/ Public Wrongs: The Liberal Lie of the Charter," *University of Toronto Law Journal* 38 (1988), p. 178. See also Andrew Petter, "The Politics of the Charter," *Supreme Court Law Review* 3 (1986), p. 472. In the British context a similar argument has been made by John Griffith, "The Rights Stuff," in Ralph Miliband and Leo Panitch, (eds.), *Real Problems, False Solutions: Socialist Register 1993* (London: Merlin Press, 1993), p. 123.
7. Recent decisions by Canadian courts extending gay and lesbian rights sparked considerable criticism of the courts as having become too political and motivated by ideology. Similar criticisms greeted the recent U.S. Supreme Court decision striking down a Texas sodomy law. See also F. Morton and R. Knopff, *The Charter Revolution and the Court Party* (Peterborough: Broadview Press, 2000). For a contrary view, see Miriam Smith,

"Ghosts of the Judicial Committee of the Privy Council: Group Politics and Charter Litigation in Canadian Political Science," *Canadian Journal of Political Science* 35 (2002), p. 3–29.

8. *Schacter v. Canada* [1992] 2 S.C.R. 679.

9. *Egan v. Canada* [1995] 2 S.C.R. 513.

10. *Eldridge v. British Columbia* [1997] 3 S.C.R. 624.

11. For a discussion of remedies in these types of situations, see Carol Rogerson, "The Judicial Search for Appropriate Remedies Under the Charter: The Examples of Overbreadth and Vagueness" in Robert Sharpe (ed.), *Charter Litigation* (Toronto: Butterworths, 1987), p. 233. An exhaustive discussion of constitutional remedies can be found in Kent Roach, *Constitutional Remedies in Canada* (Aurora, Ontario: Canada Law Book, 1994).

12. There is a large body of literature on the subject of Aboriginal rights in Canada. See, for example, John Borrows, "Contemporary Traditional Equality: The Effect of the Charter on First Nations Politics," in David Schneiderman and Kate Sutherland (eds.), *Charting the Consequences: The Impact of Charter Rights on Canadian Law and Politics* (Toronto: University of Toronto Press, 1997), p. 169–99; Kent McNeil, *Emerging Justice: Essays on Indigenous Rights in Canada and Australia* (Saskatoon: University of Saskatchewan Native Law Centre, 2001); Kent McNeil, "Aboriginal Governments and the *Canadian Charter of Rights and Freedoms*," *Osgoode Hall Law Journal* 34 (1996), p. 61–99.

13. *Canadian Charter of Rights and Freedoms*, s. 23.

14. For a discussion of these measures see Leo Panitch and Donald Swartz, *From Consent to Coercion: The Assault on Trade Union Freedoms,* 3rd edition (Toronto: Garamond Press, 2003), and Errol Black and Jim Silver, *Building a Better World: An Introduction to Unionism in Canada* (Halifax: Fernwood, 2001).

15. Reference re *Public Service Employment Relations Act (Alta.)* [1987] 1 S.C.R. 313; *PSAC v. Canada* [1987] 1 S.C.R. 424; *RWDSU v. Saskatchewan* [1987] 1 S.C.R. 460.

16. Michael McCann and Helena Silverstein, "Social Movements and the American State: Legal Mobilization as a Strategy for Democratization," in Greg Albo, David Langille and Leo Panitch, *A Different Kind of State? Popular Power and Democratic Administration* (Toronto: Oxford University Press, 1993), p. 131–43 at 133.

17. Ibid, p. 135.

18. *Brown v. Board of Education* (1954) 347 U.S. 483.

19. McCann and Silverstein, supra. note 16, p. 135.

20. See Sherene Razack, *Canadian Feminism and the Law: the Women's Legal Education and Action Fund and the Pursuit of Equality* (Toronto: Second Story Press, 1991); Elizabeth Schneider, "The Dialectics of Rights and Politics: Perspectives from the Women's Movement," *New York University Law Review* 61 (1986), p. 589–652.

21. Janine Brodie, Shelly Gavigan and Jane Jenson, *The Politics of Abortion* (Toronto: Oxford University Press, 1992).

22. Neil Milner, "The Dilemmas of Legal Mobilization: Ideologies and Strategies of Mental Patient Liberation Groups" *Law and Policy* 8 (1988), p. 105–29.

23. Carol Aylward, *Canadian Critical Race Theory: Racism and the Law* (Halifax: Fernwood Publishing, 1999).

24. Miriam Smith, *Lesbian and Gay Rights in Canada: Social Movements and Equality-Seeking, 1971–1995* (Toronto: University of Toronto Press, 1999).

25. See the activities of the Canadian Environmental Law Association, <www.cela.ca>.

26. *Roe v. Wade* (1973) 410 U.S. 113.

27. In the Canadian context, the federal division of powers meant that invalidating the criminal law prohibition on abortion in Morgentaler made the issue a health care responsibility and a matter of provincial jurisdiction. This necessitated considerable organizing and a new political campaign by abortion rights activists. See Brodie, Gavigan and Jenson, supra. note 21.

28. See Lynn Mather and Barbara Yngvesson, "Language, Audience and the Transformation of Disputes," *Law and Society* 15 (1980), p. 775.

29. Edward Hudson, "We Have a Duty to Disobey," *Winnipeg Free Press*, Sunday, March 2, 2003.

30. As a tactic, the Unregistered Firearms Association has begun to show up to protest at the court appearances of individuals charged with possessing an unregistered firearm. "Gun-Registry Foes in PM's Riding Back Accused" *Winnipeg Free Press*, March 4, 2003.

31. *Operation Dismantle v. The Queen* [1985] 1 S.C.R. 441. The case involved an application by the disarmament movement to prevent the testing of American cruise missiles in Canada on the grounds that the tests would endanger Canadians' security, contrary to section 7 of the Charter, by increasing the possibility of nuclear war.

32. McCann and Silverstein, supra. note 16, p. 137.

33. This approach has been put forward by Brian Slattery, "A Theory of the Charter," *Osgoode Hall Law Review* 25 (1987), p. 701. It is also reflected in the notion that courts and legislatures are involved in a "dialogue." In this approach, court decisions are simply moments in the policy process or statements to which governments and legislatures may respond. See Janet Hiebert, "Wrestling with Rights: Judges, Parliament and the Making of Social Policy," *Choices* 5 (1999), p. 3–32.

34. I made the argument that policymakers in the health care field must begin to incorporate rights analysis into the policy development process in B. Sheldrick, "Judicial Review and the Allocation of Health Care Resources in Canada and the United Kingdom," *Journal of Comparative Policy Analysis: Research and Practice* 5 (2003), p. 147–64.

35. See *R. v. Oakes*, [1986] 1 S.C.R. 103 and *R. v. Edward's Books and Art* [1986]

2 S.C.R. 713 for judicial discussions of the meaning of section 1. For an excellent discussion of section 1, see Janet Hiebert, *Limiting Rights: The Dilemma of Judicial Review* (Montreal: McGill-Queen's University Press, 1996).

36. James Kelly, "Bureaucratic Activism and the Charter of Rights and Freedoms: The Department of Justice and its Entry into the Centre of Government," *Canadian Public Administration* 42 (1999), p. 476–511.

37. McCann and Silverstein, supra. note 16, p. 139. This is an argument that is frequently made in support of judicial restraint.

38. For a discussion of how a rights discourse has resulted in very different judicial approaches to reviewing resource allocation decisions in the health care field, see Sheldrick, "Judicial Review and the Allocation of Health Care Resources in Canada and the United Kingdom," supra. note 37.

39. *Doucet-Boudreau v. Nova Scotia* (Minister of Education) [2003] SCC 62 (Supreme Court of Canada).

40. For a discussion of the limited effectiveness of remedies in school busing cases, see P. Gewirtz, "Remedies and Resistance," *Yale Law Journal* 92 (1983), p. 585.

41. This may have much to do with the ideology of the particular social action group before the courts. The U.S. Supreme Court recently ruled that injunctions preventing anti-abortion activists from picketing abortion clinics violated their rights to engage in dissent. See Doug Saunders, "U.S. Top Court Backs Anti-Abortion Activists," *Globe and Mail*, Feb. 27, 2003, p. A14. See *Scheidler v. National Organization for Women, Inc.*, U.S. Supreme Court, Feb. 16, 2003, available at <supct.law.cornell.edu/supct/html/01-1118.ZS.html>.

42. Hutchinson and Petter, supra. note 6.

43. *R. v. Morgentaler* [1988] 1 S.C.R. 30.

44 . See Jim Stanford, "'Third Way' Can't Survive Tony Blair," *Globe and Mail*, March 24, 2003, p. A13, for an assessment of the impact of the labour government on public services, taxation rates and poverty in Great Britain. See also Byron Sheldrick, "The Contradictions of Welfare to Work: Social Security Reform in Britain," *Studies in Political Economy* 62 (2000), p. 99–122, and Colin Leys, *Market Driven Politics Neoliberal Democracy and the Public Interest* (London: Verso, 2001).

Chapter 5

Going to Court

Often, going to court is understood simply in terms of hiring a lawyer. There are, however, a host of tactical problems and procedural issues that can significantly affect the outcome. Success or failure in court, as well as the strategic choices made along the way, can also affect the group's capacity to pursue its political agenda in other forums. Some of the important considerations involve relatively technical issues, such as how an action is started, types of lawsuits, standing and intervenor status and legal costs.[1] Yet it is far too easy to dismiss such issues as "something the lawyer will take care of." Social action groups need to understand the implications of these issues to assess whether litigation should be pursued. A good understanding of the mechanics of going to court will also better enable the group to hold its lawyers accountable and ensure that legal representation does not become legal co-optation.

Preliminary Considerations: Parties, Standing and Intervenors

One of the first questions to be asked is whether the group should be involved in litigation as a "party." Common law legal systems operate on an adversarial, party-based model. This means that the responsibility for bringing evidence before the courts rests with the parties to the litigation. The theory is that the two parties, each putting forward the strongest possible case in their favour, will ensure that all relevant information is brought to the court. This, in turn, will enhance the likelihood of the court coming to a "correct" (and one hopes just) decision. Of course, there are many problems with the adversarial model, not the least of which is that the parties may not be equally matched in their capacity to pursue litigation.

There are two basic ways to become a party: one can either commence litigation oneself, thereby becoming the plaintiff in an action, or one can be sued, thereby becoming the defendant.[2] There are a number of variations on the usual two-party situation. In some instances more than one person might be sued by the plaintiff. In other instances, additional parties might be named or "joined" to the litigation in a counterclaim

Limits of Intervenor Status

The limitations on intervenor status are well demonstrated by the events following the Ontario Court of Appeal decision in *Halpern et al. v. Attorney General of Canada* (Ont. C.A., 2003-06-10). In that case the court ruled that federal law defining marriage solely as the union of a man and a woman violated the equality rights of same-sex couples. The federal government decided not to appeal the decision to the Supreme Court of Canada. A large number of groups had intervened in the hearing of the case. Two of the groups opposed to the idea of same-sex marriage, the Association for Marriage and the Family in Ontario and the Interfaith Coalition on Marriage and Family, sought leave from the Supreme Court of Canada to be added as parties to the action and given the right to appeal the decision of the Court of Appeal. The Supreme Court of Canada denied the request on October 9, 2003.

brought by the defendant. The "joined" party is just an additional defendant in the action who is being sued by the original defendant, but not by the original plaintiff. The possible litigation scenarios can be quite complex. In most instances a social action group using litigation as a political tool will be one of the originating parties, and in many instances, the plaintiff. Where groups or individuals have been prosecuted under the criminal law or charged under provincial legislation, they will be the defendant.

There are instances, however, where a social action group may be neither of these. Rather, they may choose to intervene in a dispute between other parties. Although it is possible to intervene and seek to be added as a party to the litigation, most intervenors will do so as an *amicus curiae* or friend of the court.[3] In this context, intervention is a device by which a group or individual makes representations to the court on the interpretation of the law, but does not have the same rights as parties to the litigation. Most particularly, an intervenor will not have the right to question witnesses or present evidence to the court. They also do not have the right to appeal a decision of the court. The courts generally view it as inappropriate to permit a "stranger" to the litigation to force the original parties to continue litigating through appellate stages when they might have been content with the decision at the trial stage. Another limitation on intervenors is that they have no right to be involved in settlement negotiations. If the original parties choose to settle the issue on terms that the intervenor does not like, the intervenor has no say in the matter.

Intervenors frequently seek leave to make arguments to the courts in situations where the outcome of a decision, while perhaps not directly affecting the interests of the group, will have implications for its members or for how the law will be interpreted in future cases. In the case of *Andrews v. The Law Society of British Columbia*, for example, the Women's Legal Education and Action Fund (LEAF) was granted intervenor status, despite the fact that the case did not raise any women's issues.[4] The group wanted to intervene in *Andrews* because the Supreme Court was to interpret for the first time the equality rights contained in section 15 of the Charter. As such, this was an important opportunity for LEAF to influence the interpretation so as to achieve good outcomes in future cases more directly related to women's interests.

However, a group will not automatically be granted intervenor status. This is within the discretion of the judge and the decision depends on a number of factors. Generally courts are loath to grant intervenor status unless the potential intervenor has a real or legitimate interest in the case and can bring a perspective to the deliberations that would otherwise be lacking. If one of the parties can adequately represent the intervenor's position, the court will likely not grant intervenor status.[5]

Courts are also reluctant to grant intervenor status if the addition of intervenors would unduly complicate the proceedings. The court's concern here is with the original party litigants and with ensuring that the presence of intervenors does not make the proceedings too lengthy, complex and/or more costly. Consequently, the likelihood of being granted intervenor status may depend on the nature of the case and the stage of proceedings.

In criminal law matters it is unusual to grant intervenor status, particularly at the trial level. The primary concern for the courts is determining the accused's guilt, and the consequences for the accused can be quite serious. Criminal cases often involve a very narrow range of issues that can be dealt with by the accused and the prosecutor. There have been notable exceptions. Women's groups, for example, have succeeded at gaining intervenor status in cases involving sexual assault and domestic violence in order to provide context and perspective. This has been particularly true where the accused has attacked the constitutionality of legislative provisions safeguarding the rights of sexual assault victims.[6]

It is also relatively rare for intervenor status to be granted in civil law matters involving commercial disputes. The courts view these matters as inherently private in nature and raising only issues of financial compensation between the parties. However, it is easy to imagine a trade union wanting to intervene in a corporate bankruptcy proceeding or in litigation over a breach of contract where the outcome could mean layoffs for workers. Courts are unwilling to allow the scope of these matters to be broadened and potentially politicized.

Intervention is most frequently granted for limited purposes during a trial or during appeal hearings. For example, during a trial, intervenor

status might be granted for the limited purpose of addressing the constitutional validity of a particular law. By restricting participation in this way,
the intervenor is granted some input on matters of importance, but is
prevented from speaking to the actual liability and/or culpability of the
parties before the court. Intervenors are frequently granted status to
participate in appeal cases, particularly where those cases raise broad issues
of human rights.

These tendencies are well documented in Gregory Hein's study of
interest group litigation in Canada.[7] In cases where organized interests
seek private benefits, the overwhelming tendency is to bring an action as
a party. Only 13 percent of organized interests appearing before the
Supreme Court of Canada in these sorts of cases do so as intervenors, while
31 percent appear as parties. Before the Federal Court of Canada the
numbers are even more telling, with only 6 percent of interest groups
appearing as intervenors and 50 percent appearing as parties. Where
organized interests seek public benefits, however, the story is very
different. In these cases 69 percent of interest groups make their appearance before the Supreme Court of Canada as intervenor while only 6
percent appear as parties.[8] In private law cases it is much more difficult to
gain intervenor status and consequently, interest groups must enter
litigation as parties. In cases raising public law issues, such as human rights
and civil liberties cases, there is much broader scope for intervention,
particularly at the upper appellate levels.[9]

Advantages as Intervenor

There may be a number of advantages to participating in the judicial forum
as an intervenor. First, intervention demands a significantly smaller
commitment of resources compared to pursuing a case as a party. The
limited role of intervenors also has the advantage of insulating them from
cost awards that may be made against the parties to the litigation.[10]

Intervenors can also direct their participation to the issues of most
concern to the group. There is no need to participate in every stage of the
proceedings or to respond to every issue raised. Indeed, a group might
choose to intervene only at the level of the Supreme Court. The risk in
such a strategy is that the lower court proceedings may structure the issues
on appeal in a way that makes it difficult, or even impossible, for the group
to raise its concerns. There is also, of course, the possibility that the case
will not be appealed. On balance, however, these risks may be worth
taking given the considerable cost savings of hiring a lawyer for only one
stage of the proceedings.

Choosing an intervention strategy may also permit the group to participate in a wider range of cases. In common law legal systems, the law tends to evolve in an incremental fashion as decisions are made in individual cases. Consequently, to affect the direction of the law, it may be necessary to participate in a number of cases. For example, if a group is interested in equality law, it may have to participate in cases that do not involve its group members to ensure that the law evolves in a fashion that will ultimately be advantageous to the group. Having secured victories, it may also be necessary to participate in cases that threaten those gains or that could undermine favourable interpretations of the law. Intervention is an effective way of doing this. However, to pursue such a strategy requires a relatively sophisticated system for monitoring cases moving through the courts. There needs to be a mechanism for identifying cases of relevance to the group and for assessing whether it would be worthwhile to pursue intervention.

Different groups may operate in different ways to achieve this goal. Some might choose to have a legal affairs committee that is responsible for monitoring cases. Some might rely on loosely affiliated law centres or law foundations. Others might choose to operate more informally, relying on group members from across the country to bring forward potential cases as they become aware of them. The success of this sort of informal mechanism depends on having a mobilized membership that represents all regions of the country. Clearly, more institutionalized and well-resourced groups will be better able to carry out this strategy in a coherent and consistent fashion. Grassroots organizations and those with a relatively loose and unorganized membership will intervene more sporadically and with less consistency. They will also tend to focus on cases that have more obvious and direct implications for the group, rather than trying to shape the court's interpretation of the law over a longer period.

Standing in Court

If the group chooses to launch a lawsuit itself, the question of standing— who is entitled to bring a lawsuit before the courts—arises. Generally, only those with a direct interest, in the sense that they have suffered some injury or damage, are entitled to bring a case before the courts. Of course, the precise rules of standing vary depending on the particular issue and area of law involved. In the law of contract, for example, only those who are "privy" (i.e., parties) to the contract may sue over its breach. While a breach of a contract may affect others beyond the parties, those individuals are considered too distant from the issue before the court to be permitted to sue. The rules of standing are designed to limit the number of people coming before the court and to ensure that the courts are not inundated with claims by so-called "busybodies."

Where the litigant is a public interest group, standing sometimes becomes problematic. In many instances a social movement organization will not have standing to bring a case before the courts in its own name, because the group itself has not suffered any injury or damage. For this reason, social action groups often try to find an individual whose situation reflects the issues they are trying to raise. An anti-poverty group seeking to block cuts to welfare programs, for example, might seek an individual who has been adversely affected by the changes. If the welfare changes particularly affect particular groups of people—women, the disabled, refugees—it would be desirable to have an individual from one of these groups act as plaintiff.

Finding an individual to serve as the focus of the litigation is one of the most important and difficult things the group will need to do.[11] The facts of that individual's circumstances must effectively highlight the issues the group is trying to raise, both in general and legal terms. In a general sense, the individual needs to be sympathetic, someone with whom the broader public will identify. The individual's story needs to be compelling and "newsworthy." At the same time, the individual's circumstances must allow the group to advance the best possible case before the courts. Finally the individual needs to be committed to the project and willing to stay with it to completion. The commitment involved should not be under-estimated. Seeing a case through to the highest appeal court could take years, with periods of intense media and public scrutiny.

The task of finding an individual should not be rushed and ideally should only take place after the group has consulted its lawyers and carefully researched the project. The group needs to understand the legal issues that will be raised in court and the sort of factual context that would best advance the case. Of course, it may be very difficult to find an appropriate litigant. This is a greater dilemma for groups representing the poor and less organized than it is for social movements with a more professional and organized membership. Welfare recipients, for example, while fighting for benefits that are of immense importance to their day-to-day survival, are rarely willing or able to engage in a prolonged legal battle. For these individuals, the immediate need to secure resources for survival makes this sort of commitment difficult without tremendous external support. It is not surprising, therefore, that relatively few cases raising issues of poverty, welfare benefits or homelessness reach the highest appellate levels. These issues, when litigated, tend to take place before administrative tribunals or at lower court levels.

In some instances, a group may have little choice as to its representative. Circumstances will simply present an individual fitting the group's agenda and needing support. A group has little say about who is charged by the police, threatened with deportation or denied access to services. In these instances the group has to assess whether the facts of the case presenting itself are worth the expenditure in time and resources. Having said that, the group may feel it has little option but to come to the individual's aid and may find itself going down a litigation road that, in the best of all worlds, it might avoid.[12]

In some instances, a group may pursue litigation in its own name, without an individual "fronting" the case. This raises a somewhat more difficult set of standing issues. Historically it has been very difficult for individuals or groups to establish standing in order to litigate "in the public interest." This sort of problem comes up where a group seeks to challenge the validity of a law of general application, or in situations where it is very difficult to quantify or substantiate the damage or injury a specific individual has suffered.

In these instances, the challenge is more than simply finding an affected individual to serve as plaintiff. The nature of the case may be that there is no such individual. This is often the case in environmental matters. For example, should a government decide to allow logging in national parks where previously it was prohibited, many individuals' use and enjoyment of the park will be adversely affected. However, it may be difficult to say that the injury suffered by any particular person is different from the injury suffered by every other member of the public. Courts have frequently refused standing simply because there was a matter of public concern that required redress. Rather the courts insisted that parties must have suffered some damage unique to them to be granted standing. If the injury was of the same sort suffered by all other members of the public, then this was of public concern and standing would likely not be granted.

In public interest cases of this sort, it was generally the responsibility of the Attorney General, as an officer of the court, to bring the matter to judicial attention.[13] The position of Attorney General is somewhat unique in that this individual is both a member of cabinet and an officer of the court.[14] The common law position was that the Attorney General's responsibility for ensuring that laws were validly enacted included safeguarding the public interest. Consequently, where no individual had

Standing, Remedies, and Actual Injury

In *Steel Co. aka Chicago Steel & Pickling Co.* v. *Citizens for a Better Environment* 523 U.S. 83 (1998), the U.S. Supreme Court considered the standing of an environmental group. Citizens for a Better Environment was seeking a declaration that Chicago Steel had violated requirements to file toxic and hazardous chemical storage reports, an order authorizing the periodic inspection of the company's facilities and records, and copies of all compliance reports. By the time the case reached the courts, the company had complied with the legislative reporting requirements. The U.S. Supreme Court ruled that the environmental group lacked standing in the case. It held that standing required three elements: i) actual injury to the plaintiff, ii) a causal link between the defendant's actions and the plaintiff's injury and iii) that the remedy requested redresses that injury. The court took the view that the remedies sought were oriented to preventing future breaches of the law, rather than providing relief for any injury or damage caused by the original late reporting. Consequently, it ruled that even if it could be shown that Citizens for a Better Environment, or its members, had suffered actual injury, the group still lacked standing.

standing to challenge a law, the Attorney General would, in theory, step in to fill the void. The decision as to whether or not to go to court in the public interest, however, was the Attorney General's and was completely beyond challenge or review.[15] Of course, given the dictates of modern parliamentary government and the demands of cabinet solidarity, it is hardly surprising that the Attorney General could rarely be relied upon to put aside partisan and governmental needs and pursue litigation challenging her own government's actions.

A similarly restrictive position on standing for social interest groups exists in the U.S., where the Supreme Court ruled that a plaintiff must show actual or threatened injury before standing is granted. Even where this can be done, the court has a discretion to deny standing if the plaintiff raises "abstract questions of wide public significance."[16] It rejected the notion that every citizen should be entitled to go to court simply to test the constitutional validity of laws. It held that a broad public interest standing rule would bring the courts into conflict with the legislature over the validity of laws in situations where no one had suffered any "cognizable injury" or harm.

In Canada, the limited capacity of social action groups to gain standing and the obvious inadequacy of relying on the Attorney General eventually produced judicial reform. In a series of cases that became known as the "standing trilogy," the Supreme Court of Canada significantly expanded the scope of public interest standing in constitutional cases.[17] As a result, standing rules in Canada are now among the most liberal in the western world.[18] While the court might still prefer to grant standing to individuals with a direct interest in the litigation, public interest standing will nevertheless be granted provided a number of conditions are met. Essentially, the plaintiff must satisfy the court that:

a)   the case raises a serious issue regarding the validity of the legislation;
b)   if not directly affected by the legislation, the plaintiff has a genuine interest in its validity; and
c)   there is no other reasonable and effective way to bring the matter before the court.[19]

These conditions are designed separate out the "busy-body" from the genuine public interest litigant raising a serious constitutional issue where no directly affected individuals are available to bring the case forward.

The Project Loophole litigation, in which the Manitoba group CHO!CES challenged a Revenue Canada decision allowing a wealthy Canadian family to move a $2 billion trust fund out of the country without paying taxes, is a good example of how these standing rules operate.[20] Since the group was not incorporated and did not pay taxes, the decision was made not to bring the litigation in the group's name, but rather in the name of one of its members—George Harris. As a community activist and taxpayer, Harris had a history of concern with social issues and a genuine interest in ensuring that Canada's tax laws were applied correctly. Moreover, there was no other way for the issue to come before the court. While Harris was clearly not directly affected by Revenue Canada's decision, there was no party who could be reasonably expected to litigate the matter. Neither Revenue Canada, which made the decision, nor the family that benefited from it could be expected to go to court over the matter. Since there were no other directly affected parties, there was no mechanism, other than a concerned citizen, for bringing the matter to the courts.

The requirement that there be no other reasonable and effective way to bring the matter to court, however, clearly demonstrates the court's preference for individual litigants who have, in the words of the U.S. Supreme Court, suffered a "cognizable injury." Moreover, under the Supreme Court of Canada's formulation, the existence of potential litigants who have suffered direct injury is sufficient to disqualify a public interest litigant from standing, even if the individuals do not wish to litigate the issue. From the court's perspective, if those affected do not wish to challenge the legislation, then the harm they have suffered must be considered fairly insignificant. In this context it is not for some other group to step into their shoes and take the case forward. This approach, however, ignores the social and economic factors that may prevent an individual from pursuing litigation and raises the possibility that potentially unconstitutional laws will be left on the books simply for want of an individual to challenge them.

Standing rules make it particularly difficult for social action groups to challenge a broad-based law or policy. The broader the basis of the challenge, the more difficult it will generally be to say that no individuals exist who could bring forward a challenge to the legislation themselves. If an individual brings a case forward, however, it is unlikely that the scope of the challenge would be as broad. Rather, an individual plaintiff would likely raise issues with respect to specific sections or specific details of the legislative scheme rather than to the entire legislation. This introduces the possibility that, even if successful, the court might invalidate parts of the legislation, while leaving the rest in force. For the social action group, then, it might be necessary to bring several cases, each with an individual plaintiff, to have the same impact as would be achieved by bringing the case in the group's own name.

This problem is demonstrated by the decision of the Supreme Court of Canada in *The Canadian Council of Churches v. The Queen*.[21] The Canadian Council of Churches, through its Inter-Church Committee for Refugees, had a long history of advocacy on behalf of refugee claimants. The Council sought to challenge the constitutional validity of amendments to the *Immigration Act* on the basis that the changes to the refugee determination process would violate the rights of refugees under the *Canadian Charter of Rights and Freedoms*. The court, however, ruled that the Council did not qualify for public interest standing on the grounds that individual refugee claimants could challenge those aspects of the legislation that allegedly violated their rights. The Council would be free to seek intervenor status in those cases to raise the public interest issues about which it had expertise. Instead of a single case examining the constitutionality of the amendments, therefore, a series of cases testing each proposed amendment would be required. From the court's perspective, this is preferable since each case will have a factual background and context, which would be lacking if the case were carried forward by the public interest group. From the group's perspective, however, this makes litigation potentially unworkable as a political strategy since the costs, difficulties of case selection and recruitment of plaintiffs are multiplied considerably.

It should be noted that the original standing trilogy extended public interest standing only to constitutional cases. In the subsequent case of

Finlay v. Canada (Minister of Finance),[22] which involved a challenge to the administration of federal-provincial shared-cost programs in the area of welfare, the Supreme Court of Canada extended public interest standing beyond constitutional cases to other situations where an individual or group is seeking to challenge the statutory authority of an administrative action. As a result, there is now quite a broad scope for a social action group to argue for standing as a public interest litigant, although the need to demonstrate that there is no suitable individual plaintiff can still be a difficult obstacle to overcome.

Costs of Litigation

The costs of litigation can be very great. In the *Finlay* case, for example, the initial court decision on Finlay's standing was appealed to the Supreme Court of Canada, which ruled in Finlay's favour. The case was sent back to the lower courts for a trial on the issues, and was again appealed to the Supreme Court. The original trial court decision on the standing issue was delivered on November 17, 1982. The Supreme Court ruled on the standing issue in the case in 1986 and the final Supreme Court decision in the case was released in 1993, over a decade after the case began. It is critical, therefore, that the financial costs of litigation be taken into account by any social action group contemplating involvement in a court case. Pursuing a case through trial and the appellate level will take a very long time and cost a great deal. Moreover, if a number of preliminary issues, such as a challenge to the group's standing are raised, the case might be delayed considerably. While *Finlay* may be exceptional, a group must be prepared for the long haul if it wishes to pursue this strategy.

It is difficult to estimate with any precision how much a lawsuit will cost. The length of the case, the complexity of the issues, the need for expert witnesses, the preparation of scientific or technical reports and variations in lawyers' fees will all affect the total cost. Senior partners, for example, charge more than junior lawyers, while lawyers in Toronto or New York charge more than lawyers in Winnipeg or Rochester. The Canadian government's Court Challenges Program, which provides funding in equality and minority language rights cases, will provide a maximum of $50,000 for a trial and $35,000 for an appeal.[23] In most instances litigation costs will be significantly greater than this. To take a case all the way to the Supreme Court of Canada will likely cost in excess of several hundred thousand dollars.

Financing such an endeavour may be difficult.[24] It may be possible to find a lawyer willing to take a public interest case on a pro bono basis, foregoing her usual fee and providing service as an act of charity. Lawyers are reluctant to take on such cases, however, particularly if a case is going to be very expensive to finance or is complex and requires a large investment of staff time. Law firms are in the business of selling legal skills to make a profit and there is little monetary profit in charity. Moreover, given that many lawyers will be unwilling, relying on pro bono representation necessarily means limiting the selection of lawyers. Only very large firms will be able to take on an expensive constitutional challenge. It may be, however, that these lawyers are less committed to the ideological project of the group than lawyers in smaller "boutique" or specialized law firms. The firm itself may impose some restrictions on the number and nature of cases it is willing to take on.[25]

Another option is legal aid. All Canadian provinces run their own legal aid systems; similar programs also exist in the United States and Britain. In Canada, most legal aid systems operate on some version of an indemnity plan for legal costs. The plan pays lawyers directly on behalf of individuals unable to afford to hire a lawyer themselves. The individual applies for legal aid and, if approved, receives a voucher or certificate for her lawyer to claim payment from the plan. The amount that a lawyer may charge is set by the legal aid plan and is usually considerably lower than what can be charged for non-legal aid cases. Consequently, many lawyers are reluctant to take on legal aid cases, particularly for complex matters, since, in the long run, they divert resources away from more financially lucrative cases. Many lawyers find it increasingly difficult to make a living and cover the overhead costs of running a legal practice while relying on legal aid casework.[26]

Over the past decade, legal aid plans have endured extreme financial pressures. In addition to low tariffs, the range of cases covered by legal aid plans has narrowed. In fact, legal aid was never intended for all types of cases. It was intended primarily to ensure that individuals charged with criminal offences had representation. It has also been generally available for a limited number of family law matters. Civil law cases, as well as appearances before administrative tribunals and agencies, are usually beyond the scope of many legal aid systems. In other words, legal aid was reserved for what the legal profession considered some of the most serious legal issues, but it never provided the poor with a full range of legal services. As funding has been constrained, so too has the range of cases funded by legal aid.

Consequently, legal aid is likely a limited resource for most social movements. First, the plaintiff must meet the income requirements of the legal aid plan. Then, the specific case must fit into a category for which funding is provided. Obviously, legal aid will be particularly beneficial in those situations where an individual has been charged by the police. Most legal aid plans do not fund test case litigation. Ontario is an exception.

It may also be possible to utilize the services of a community legal clinic. Ontario has a network of seventy-eight community-based legal clinics. Although funded by the legal aid plan, each clinic has an independent board of directors, which sets, within certain limitations, the priorities of that clinic. Many are general service clinics with a specialization in poverty law. They tend to focus on welfare law, landlord and tenant law, unemployment insurance issues and other matters of particular concern to low income individuals. Other clinics, however, specialize in a particular area of the law or the needs of a particular community. For example, clinics may be devoted to environmental law, tenant issues, family law or workers' compensation. Specialty clinics focusing on communities may deal with the problems faced by the disabled, the elderly, the African community, refugees, Aboriginal people or

In-Kind Contributions and Negotiating Fee Arrangements

In some instances it may be possible to negotiate a fee arrangement with a legal clinic or law foundation based on a group's ability to pay. In the Project Loophole litigation, legal services were provided by the Public Interest Law Centre. The Centre was established in 1982 as a branch of Manitoba Legal Aid and undertakes test case litigation on behalf of individuals and groups. CHOICES, the anti-poverty coalition that sponsored the Project Loophole litigation, negotiated a fee with the Public Interest Law Centre based on the group's ability to pay. This amount represented only a portion of the total legal costs, with the remainder being covered by the Public Interest Law Centre. In effect, the Law Centre made a significant "in-kind" contribution to the group's efforts. Project Loophole relied on donations from members of the public and other fundraising techniques to cover these costs.

There are frequently many possibilities for "in-kind" contributions that can offset the potential costs of litigation. The writing of new releases and promotional material may be done by members of the group, local law professors might volunteer legal expertise and help translate legal information into a more accessible form, and individuals may volunteer to conduct a host of direct action events.

individuals with HIV-AIDS.[27] The mandate of these specialty clinics often includes the pursuit of test cases on behalf of their particular constituency. Such clinics provide their services free of charge, although there may be income qualification requirements in some instances. While no other jurisdiction in Canada has a clinic system comparable to Ontario's, most jurisdictions have some organizations or institutions that fulfil a similar function and may help pursue a case before the courts. Links to these organizations can be found in Appendix 1. It needs to be kept in mind, however, that most of these organizations are extremely under-resourced and the demands for their services are very high.

In Canada, another important source of funds for litigation is the Court Challenges Program, a national non-profit organization that provides financial assistance for test cases raising equality rights or language rights issues under the *Canadian Charter of Rights and Freedoms*. As such, the program, which is administered by the Department of Canadian Heritage, is limited in the range of cases that it supports, but nevertheless it does provide an important avenue for equality-seeking groups and official minority language groups to pursue cases before the courts. In addition to funding litigation, the program also provides funding for case develop-ment work, including community consultations, impact studies on the possible effects of a court decision and program promotion. This final category includes funding for national and regional meetings/conferences and consultations that enhance the capacity of groups to use of the Court Challenges Program.

While the funding provided by the Court Challenges Program is important, it is also limited and is provided directly to the group or individual, which must then account for its expenditure. In addition, the maximum allowable amounts are quite low.[28] For example, the program will not provide more than $35,000 for an appeal, and will fund lawyers' fees to a maximum amount of $150 per hour for court appearances. In many parts of Canada, articling students bill at close to this rate and senior lawyers charge $300 or more per hour for their services. The Court Challenges Program, then, while an important supplement, doesn't eliminate the need for the group to engage in additional fundraising efforts.

Officials in the Court Challenges Program recognize the limits of the funding they are able to offer groups. To this end, the program has asked groups receiving funding to assist in documenting the resource imbalance that exists between plaintiffs and the government. Program officials have also asked participants to report instances where the government explicitly takes a position contrary to equality rights and where the government attempts to use procedural motions and delay as tactics. These tactics increase the costs of litigation to a cash-strapped plaintiff and could result in the case being abandoned.

Cost Awards by the Court

In assessing the potential financial implications of litigation, it is important to remember that courts frequently impose cost awards at the end of the case. This means that in addition to paying your own legal costs, you may also be responsible for a portion of your opponent's legal costs. Judicial rules about costs vary from jurisdiction to jurisdiction, but three broad types of systems exist. Courts in the United States employ what is sometimes referred to as a "no way" rule in which each side is responsible for paying its own costs. In the United Kingdom, on the other hand, a system of "costs in the cause" requires the losing party to pay most of the costs of the winning party. The rationale underpinning this approach is that the losing party should compensate the winner for the expenses involved in litigation. If the loser had not contested the case, the winner would not have incurred those costs. It is a damage award model in which costs are designed to put the winning party in relatively the same position as if the litigation had not taken place. The British approach is also designed to discourage people from litigating in the absence of a strong case, whereas the American approach tends to make it easier for people to bring cases before the courts.

In Canada, a system of "party and party" costs is employed. Under this approach the loser must pay a portion of the winner's costs based on a tariff established by the rules of civil procedure in the particular provincial jurisdiction. This approach seeks a middle ground between the American and British models and is designed to encourage the settlement of disputes, without limiting access to the courts.[29] It is important to remember that awarding costs is completely within the discretion of the court. In public interest cases, judges occasionally decline to award costs against a losing party, particularly if the defendant is the government. In other instances, if the winning party is the Attorney General, it may be possible for the loser to negotiate with the government and achieve a reduction in costs. However, counting on the good will of the government in these cases is inadvisable and, overall, courts tend not to distinguish between public interest litigants and other types of parties when awarding costs.[30]

It should also be kept in mind that some type of advance fund to satisfy a potential cost award may be necessary. Under Canadian rules of civil procedure the defendant is entitled to ask for "security for costs" when there is reason to believe the plaintiff does not have sufficient assets to pay a cost award or where the litigation is "frivolous and vexatious."[31] There are good reasons for a defendant to apply for security of costs. On the one hand, it stalls the litigation. More importantly, however, if the plaintiff cannot afford to pay the security, a successful motion may effectively halt the litigation before it even begins.[32]

Contingency Fees

When hiring a lawyer a deposit is required on the total cost of legal services. This is referred to as a "retainer." If the case is going to continue over an extended period of time, the lawyer will likely issue periodic billings. One way to avoid these initial and ongoing costs is through a contingency fee arrangement, whereby the lawyer and the client agree that payment will be made at the end of the litigation from any damage award or compensation that the plaintiff receives. More significantly, in a contingency fee arrangement lawyers agree to waive their fees if the case is unsuccessful. Contingency fees are widely used in the United States, but are a relatively recent development in Canada. Although historically illegal here, they are now available in all provinces.[33]

Contingency fees, however, may be of limited use in a public law context because most such cases do not involve large sums of money. Such fees are only workable where there is a big enough pot of money available at the end of the litigation to compensate the lawyers. The potential rewards have to be big enough for the lawyers to gamble on winning the case and getting paid or losing and not getting paid. The outcome of most public law cases, however, involves a declaration that a statute or some other public act is invalid. In other instances it confirms the availability of a state benefit or program to a group of individuals. In such instances there is no monetary award and, consequently, lawyers would not be willing to work on a contingency fee basis.

There may be "public cases," however, where contingency fees could be employed. This would include situations where individuals or groups are suing either the government or a private company for compensation due to negligence. So-called "toxic torts," where individuals sue for damages because environmental toxins have harmed their health, are a good example. Individuals might also sue the state for compensation where a state policy or government inaction has led to harm. Aboriginal claims for damages for physical and sexual abuse resulting from the operation of residential schools is a good example of cases that involve both private organizations, such as churches, and governments as defendants. In these cases contingency fee arrangements might be workable so long as the pool of money sought is sufficiently large to both provide compensation to the plaintiffs and cover legal costs.

Class Action Lawsuits

Contingency fees are also available in class action lawsuits. Class action litigation involves a small group bringing a lawsuit on behalf of a larger group of people who stand to benefit from the litigation. Class action lawsuits are a relatively new phenomenon in Canada. Quebec was the first jurisdiction to permit class action litigation, in 1978. Ontario passed the *Class Proceedings Act* in 1992, British Columbia followed in 1995 and more recently Newfoundland and Saskatchewan enacted their own class action legislation in 2002. The Ontario legislation permits suits to be launched for the entire country. This is a departure from the normal rules of civil procedure, which generally require either the plaintiff or the defendant to reside in the jurisdiction, or the subject matter of the dispute to have arisen within the jurisdiction. Under the Ontario class action legislation, suits can be brought in the province even when the subject matter of the litigation and the parties originate from somewhere else in the country.

Class Action in the United States

Class actions are extremely common in the United States. Over the past decade there has been a steady increase in the number of class action lawsuits dealt with by federal courts:

Year	Suits Filed	Suits Ended	Total Work load
1991	930	1874	2427
1992	1196	2129	3109
1993	852	2131	2981
1994	991	2204	3122
1995	1340	2441	3544
1996	1356	2441	3797
1997	1475	2641	3916
1998	1881	3114	4522
1999	2133	3251	5247
2000	2393	3882	5644
2001	3092	4563	6975

Source: *Class Action Reports*: <www.classactionreports.com/classactionreports/stats2.htm>.

The significance of a class action suit is that it brings all potential litigants under a single umbrella. This makes the prospect of litigation more affordable from an individual standpoint. To bring a class–action suit, an application must be made to the court establishing a "class of litigants." This means that a commonality of interest must be established. Usually one or two individuals carry the suit forward and, in effect, represent the entire group of affected people. If the suit is successful, the court will then quantify damages for the entire class of litigants, which will then be apportioned amongst all those who have joined the suit. The legislation governing class action suits usually requires advertisements informing all potential plaintiffs about the suit and their right to participate. If an individual falls within the definition of the class, then she is automatically bound by the results of the litigation. This means she will share in any damage awards that result and she cannot, in the future, litigate the matter on an individual basis. The individual, however, may choose to opt out of the class action litigation, thereby preserving the right to sue independently, presumably in the hopes of receiving a larger damage award. Under Canadian legislation, individuals are automatically

Highlighting the Breadth of a Issue

One of the drawbacks of litigation is that it focuses on the individuals before the court. One of the advantages of a class action suit, therefore, is that it expands the scope of the court's attention beyond the individual litigants before it. In British Columbia, a class action lawsuit is challenging the policy of the province's jails to strip-search all people arrested and placed in a holding cell. This is the only jurisdiction in Canada with such a practice. The plaintiffs in the case include an Anglican minister who was strip-searched after being arrested during a demonstration. Another plaintiff was arrested for placing posters on bus shelters during a May Day parade. The impact of each case in demonstrating the unreasonableness of the policy is enhanced by combining them into a single class-action suit.

deemed to be part of a class and must formally opt out of the proceedings if they wish to preserve their rights to pursue their own litigation. If the litigation is unsuccessful, the members of the class are not responsible for any of the legal costs of the lawsuit and incur no financial obligations because of it.

Class action suits are very useful where a large number of individuals have been affected by either public or private action. Again, however, their utility may be limited in many public law cases. The advantage and utility of class action suits is that they are a cost-effective mechanism for providing a remedy to a large number of people, without each one having to bring her own individual lawsuit. In a public law context, however, where the remedy sought is a declaration of legislative invalidity, the great majority of affected individuals do not need to litigate to benefit from the success of a single individual plaintiff. For example, the success of recent cases seeking to have declared unconstitutional the Canadian federal law defining marriage in heterosexual terms has benefited all gays and lesbians who wish to marry, not just those who litigated.[34] There is no need for those not involved in the litigation to bring their own cases to establish their entitlement to marry. This is the essence of public law in that it provides collective remedies with implications for individuals other than those who actually appear before the court.

Choosing a Lawyer and Going to Court

Choosing a lawyer can be a difficult task. Save for the occasional routine matter such as completing a house purchase or preparing a will, most of us have very little need for the services of a lawyer. When going to court as part of a political campaign, there is a wider range of issues to address than in most litigation contexts. First, it is advantageous if the lawyer has some political commitment to the cause you are advancing. While law schools may argue that lawyers are trained to advance a position regardless of their personal viewpoint, it is extremely difficult in political litigation to separate one's ideological perspective from the case at hand. Moreover, in political litigation, positions might be taken to advance a political point, rather than strictly from an assessment of what will win the case. A lawyer committed or at least sympathetic to the cause will be better able to understand these aspects of the case and more willing to work with the organization to achieve its goals.

Social action groups that are well-established and highly institution-alized may have advantages in locating and finding this sort of individual. Lawyers may actually be members of the organization or serve on its governing board. These individuals, if unable to carry the litigation forward themselves, may recommend other lawyers sympathetic to the cause who would be willing to take the case on. If the group has a history of test case litigation, it may already have a network of lawyers to call on or even have lawyers on staff. For groups that are less institutionalized or new to the litigation game, however, finding and choosing a lawyer may be a daunting task.

A number of factors should be considered. These include the lawyer's experience and expertise, political commitment, as well as the fees for service. Generally speaking, the more experienced the lawyer, the higher the fees. At the same time, for complex litigation, a relatively inexperi-enced lawyer might not be a good choice. Having said this, highly experienced lawyers may find it more difficult to work in a collaborative fashion with a social action organization. Such individuals may be more inclined to view the group's involvement as a hindrance, or even a nuisance, and prefer to have autonomy in pursuing the case.

The Canadian Court Challenges Program lists a number of criteria that groups should consider when selecting a lawyer for constitutional test cases. These include:

- years in practice;
- amount and type of courtroom experience;
- amount and type of experience with constitutional law (or the area of law involved); and
- specialization, if any, particularly in the issues at hand.[35]

The ideal lawyer is competent, possesses the expertise and skills necessary to carry the case forward, and is well regarded both in the legal community and in the social movement community. Litigation is a specialized area of legal practice. We cannot expect a real estate lawyer, or a general practitioner who rarely appears before the courts, to handle a complex court case. At the same time, litigators also tend to specialize. A civil litigator who practices exclusively in the area of commercial litigation would not be a good choice to advance a constitutional case involving equality rights. Different lawyers may also be required at different stages of the proceedings. Some lawyers specialize in trial work, while others are experts at appeals.

There are a number of routes and vehicles for locating a lawyer. Most law societies and bar associations maintain a lawyer referral list. This can be useful but should not necessarily be relied upon. The lawyers on the list are generally not vetted by the law societies with respect to areas of specialization and/or levels of experience. Lawyers simply request that their names be added to the list. Individuals seeking a referral are provided with a number of names from the top of the list on that particular day. The lawyers might be ideal for a specific case, but at the same time, they might not.

There are, however, other resources. Legal clinics, other advocacy groups and even social action groups with litigation experience may be able to provide referrals and recommendations. Law schools also provide a valuable resource. Their Web sites list areas of specialization of faculty members. Many law professors are called to the bar and some get involved in interesting litigation, particularly in constitutional matters. Law faculty, then, may be a valuable resource. If a law professor is unwilling or unable to get involved in the actual case, she will likely recommend a suitable practising lawyer. Lawyers in many jurisdictions are now permitted to advertise, and one might find a lawyer through Internet or television promotion. Generally, however, lawyers choose not to advertise. Word of mouth and the recommendations of either group members and or other groups with whom there is a shared or common political commitment are often the most useful resources for finding a lawyer.

It is important to keep in mind that law is ultimately a service industry and the potential litigant is the customer. All lawyers are not equal and there is a tremendous range in competency. One should be completely satisfied as to the capacity, expertise and quality of one's legal representation before proceeding with a complex political case. One should also be satisfied as to the lawyer's willingness to work with a social action group rather than an individual client.

Once you have chosen a possible lawyer, you should meet with her, explain the case and get her input. The initial consultation is also an important opportunity to set out your political aspirations for the case, consider how it fits into the group's overall political agenda and gauge the lawyer's reaction to those issues. This is also the time to spell out your understanding of the nature of the lawyer-client relationship. If the group wants to be actively involved in drafting and vetting court documents, and in making tactical decisions as the litigation develops, then this is the time to make that clear. If the lawyer is uncomfortable with having an active and involved client, it should become apparent. If you are not satisfied with the outcome of that initial meeting, you should meet with other lawyers to see if another approach to the litigation is more consistent with the group's. Lawyers often provide their initial consultation free of charge. However, even if this is not the case, it is far better to pay the fee and find a new lawyer than stick with a lawyer with whom your group has difficulty working. More money will be wasted by staying with an unsuitable lawyer than by continuing the search for an appropriate one. Remember, the lawyer finally chosen is someone the group will have to work with for a potentially long period of time and someone to whom the group will pay a great deal of money.

Stages of Litigation

Litigation can be a lengthy and complicated process. The basic stages, however, are relatively straightforward and can be divided into:

Pleadings and Discovery

Pleadings are the mechanism by which a lawsuit is initiated and which provide all the parties with an opportunity to state their initial positions. The pleadings also operate to define what questions will be at issue in the trial. Parties are generally not permitted to raise issues that were not originally included in the pleadings. It is extremely important, therefore, that care be taken in crafting the pleadings.

Lawsuits are started by issuing a statement of claim. In some common law jurisdictions, this is still referred to by the somewhat antiquated term, "writ of proceeding." The statement of claim includes all the material facts upon which the case is based and the remedy being requested from the court. It is important to begin the proceedings relatively expeditiously. If there is some utility in pursuing litigation, then legal advice should also be sought fairly soon. In most jurisdictions, statutes of limitations put strict limits on the time that can pass before commencing a lawsuit. In civil actions, where the defendant is a private citizen or a corporation, the time limit is usually six years from the date on which the cause of action became known to the plaintiff. When suing public authorities, however, the limitation period can be quite a bit shorter depending on the level of government and the nature of the issue. In some instances, the plaintiff may have six months or even less to commence litigation.

It is very important in all cases, but particularly in political litigation, that the plaintiff work closely with the lawyer to craft the statement of claim. This is the means by which the political issues of concern to the group become translated into legal language. The facts as set out in the statement of claim must disclose a legal cause of action. If they do not, or if portions of the statement of claim are considered irrelevant to the advancement of the cause of action, the defendant may ask the court to strike out either the entire statement or portions of it. In a motion to have a statement of claim struck out, the court asks whether the facts as alleged in the claim entitle the plaintiff to a remedy. If the answer is no, then the statement of claim has not disclosed a sufficient cause of action and the case goes no further. Similarly, portions of the statement of claim may also be struck out if the court feels that they are irrelevant to advancing the cause of action.

This can make it difficult to include all of the political items the group might wish to raise. During the APEC demonstrations in Vancouver, for example, demonstrators were subjected to police violence and harassment. In a subsequent inquiry, the RCMP Public Complaints Commission found that the use of force by police officers had been excessive.[36] One of the issues the demonstrators wanted to raise at the hearings was the degree to which the Prime Minister's Office had been involved in planning and authorizing the quelling of the demonstrations. In addition to pursuing the hearings before the Public Complaints Commission, the demonstrators might also have sued the police officers directly for damages. However, this option might have provided less opportunity to investigate the political involvement of the Prime Minister and his staff. The question in a trial of this sort would simply have been whether or not the force used was reasonable, given the circumstances. Who authorized the use of force would likely have been viewed as irrelevant. Consequently, had the demonstrators sued and included in a statement of claim the allegation that the Prime Minister had authorized the use of force, it is likely that those sections would have been struck out by the court. Only if the demonstrators sued the Prime Minister and/or his staff directly for their involvement would these allegations have been relevant to the litigation.

Typically, a lawyer interviews a client and then draws up a statement of claim. Social action groups should try to have input into the drafting of the claim and should certainly ensure that they see a draft of the claim before it is filed. If the lawyers do not feel it is appropriate to include certain issues in the statement of claim, an explanation is required. There may be instances where a group wants to include items even if they might give rise to a motion to have portions of the claim struck out. Even if some issues do not make it to the trial, including them in the statement of claim may result in some public attention.

Once the statement of claim has been issued, the defendant must respond by filing a statement of defence. Failure to do so will lead to a summary judgement against the defendant. The statement of defence is the defendant's response to the allegations in the statement of claim. It usually involves a denial of the facts as set out in the statement of claim, although in some instances the defendant may agree on certain facts. Any facts that are admitted are subsequently accepted by the court and do not have to be proven by the plaintiff at the trial. The statement of defence may also assert additional facts

> ### Suing the Prime Minister
>
> Democracy Street, a coalition of Vancouver activists who had been involved in the APEC demonstrations did in fact launch a lawsuit directly against the Prime Minister and members of his office for their alleged involvement in the police violence at the demonstrations. The statement of claim, which can be found at <www.democracy-street.tao.ca>, cites damages for assault, false arrest and imprisonment, negligence and infringement of the demonstrators' constitutional rights. It can be very difficult to bring an action against a public official. Generally, the concept of public interest immunity prevents lawsuits from being brought against public officials for carrying out their official functions. It is frequently necessary to demonstrate that the officials were acting outside of their official capacity and/or that their actions were malicious in nature. This is even more difficult when suing members of the executive such as the Prime Minister. In many common law jurisdictions, the Prime Minister has the right not to respond to a subpoena to attend court if the lawsuit relates to her role as Prime Minister.

that were not included in the plaintiff's statement of claim. In some instances, the statement of defence may also include a counterclaim. This occurs where the defendant actually sues the plaintiff over the same issue. The counterclaim will follow the same format as a statement of claim. In some instances the defendant may bring a counterclaim in an attempt to intimidate the plaintiff by subjecting her to the risk of a large damage award. This is an example of the SLAPP phenomenon discussed in Chapter 3.

Finally, the plaintiff is given an opportunity to respond to the statement of defence. The response must be limited to accepting or denying any new facts raised by the statement of defence and any counterclaim. It cannot raise issues not included in the original statement of claim.

Sometime after the completion of pleadings and before the commencement of the trial, a process known as "discovery" takes place. During discovery all parties must disclose to the others all relevant documents and materials in their possession. There may also be an opportunity for the parties to question each other before an officer of the court. Although the answers given during discovery are not binding on the parties, nevertheless it will be difficult to explain why any testimony has changed. The objective of discovery is to ensure that the trial does not involve "ambushes" or surprises. If each party is aware of the material that the other is relying on, the possibilities for narrowing issues and/or arriving at a settlement are increased.

Some documents do not have to be turned over during discovery. Indeed, each party may claim that certain documents are privileged and can remain confidential. The most usual ground of privilege is lawyer-client confidentiality. This applies to all conversations and records of conversations between a lawyer and her client. It also applies to any documents, reports or studies that were prepared "in contemplation" of litigation. In other words, if your lawyer asks you to investigate something, or to generate some statistical information, or to commission a study or report in anticipation of being sued, those reports and information are confidential and do not have to be turned over to the plaintiff. Any other material relevant to the case, however, must be disclosed. This would include correspondence and reports or studies that were completed in the normal course of business operations.

The Trial
The trial is the vehicle by which the court gathers factual information on which to base a legal judgement. It is also the stage of proceedings that people are most familiar with, thanks to television and films. While trials may make excellent Hollywood dramas, they can actually be long and tedious affairs. The general structure of a trial is well understood. Witnesses are called to present evidence and undergo questioning by lawyers representing both the plaintiff and the defendant. The plaintiff presents her case first, followed by the defendant. At the end, the "trier of fact"—either a jury or a judge sitting alone—makes findings of fact to which relevant legal principles are applied. In Canada, most cases no longer utilize juries. This is particularly so for civil actions. Juries are still commonly used in the United States, however, particularly in large negligence cases. In both Canada and the United States, juries are more common in criminal proceedings, although even in this area of law trial by judge is increasingly the norm except in the most serious cases.

In some instances a trial may be unnecessary. "Applications for declaratory relief" and "applications for judicial review" often proceed by way of a motion. In these circumstances somewhat different terminology is employed and a different process is followed. The applicant (plaintiff) files a notice of motion on the respondent (defendant). The notice of motion serves much the same function as the statement of claim. Each party then files with the court a motion record. The motion record includes all the necessary factual material and supporting evidence for the judge to make a decision. A motion hearing is then held in which the lawyers make their arguments to the judge as to the merits of their positions. Witnesses are unusual in these proceedings. Rather, evidence is presented by way of affidavits. These are sworn written statements that are presented to the judge. If there is a disagreement about the content of an affidavit, the individual who swore it may be called before the court for cross-examination.

Two issues pertaining to trials are of vital importance. These are the "onus of proof" and the "standard of proof." An onus of proof refers to the question of who has to prove what in a trial, while standard of proof refers to the degree of certainty required. As a general rule, whoever asserts something in a trial has the onus of proving it. Consequently, in a rights case the onus is on the individual claiming a violation of her rights to demonstrate that her rights have, in fact, been violated. In other words, anyone alleging discrimination is responsible for actually proving unequal and discriminatory treatment. In a sense the onus of proof acts as a tiebreaker. If, after hearing all the evidence, the judge or jury cannot make a decision, then the individual with the onus of proof has failed to discharge her legal responsibility to convince and loses the case.[37]

This distinction is made clearer by considering standards of proof. It is one thing to say that an individual must prove or establish something, but quite another to establish how certain that proof must be. In other words, does the judge or jury have to be absolutely convinced, or just relatively convinced that something occurred. There are two standards of proof: proof on a balance of probabilities and proof beyond reasonable doubt. The latter is the standard in criminal trials and it is a demanding one. It requires that any "reasonable" doubts must be resolved in favour of the accused through an acquittal. In a self-defence case, for example, this means that the accused does not have to convince the jury that she acted in self-defence but merely raise a doubt in their minds about the issue. It is the prosecution's responsibility to present evidence that will eliminate that doubt. If the onus of proof is a tiebreaker, the standard of proof acts as a form of handicap or weighting that shifts when the parties are considered "tied."

In civil matters a lower standard of proof—proof on a balance of probabilities—is utilized. This standard simply requires that it be more likely than not that something is true. It is a much easier standard for the plaintiff to meet. At the same time, this is also the standard the defendant must meet on those issues for which it has the onus of proof. This standard of proof applies to all non-criminal litigation between private litigants— contract disputes, negligence claims, family law matters, etc. It also applies to constitutional challenges.

In constitutional cases, while the onus of proof is initially on the plaintiff to establish a rights violation on a balance of probabilities, it shifts to the state on the question of justification. Under the *Canadian Charter of Rights of Freedoms*, section 1 provides that all rights are subject to reasonable limits. The courts have adopted a two-step analysis for Charter cases. In the first step, the plaintiff/applicant establishes that a violation of rights has taken place. If successfully established on a balance of probabilities, the state then has the onus of demonstrating that the infringement of rights was reasonable and justified.

Under the Charter the courts have developed a "proportionality" test for determining the reasonableness of a rights violation. Essentially the state must demonstrate two things to the court. First, that its objectives are sufficiently important to justify a violation of rights. Second, it must demonstrate proportionality. This involves answering three questions. First, are the policy objectives and the means chosen to pursue them rationally connected? This requires that the policy instruments chosen by the state must advance, in some way, the state's original objective. If the state cannot demonstrate this connection, then it will have failed to discharge its obligation to demonstrate proportionality. The courts are not too stringent about this requirement and do not require empirically verifiable data to demonstrate the link between policy and objective. In other words, the government does not have to demonstrate that the policy will result in the achievement of its objective, only that, on balance, there appears to be some reasonable linkage between the two.

The final stages of the proportionality inquiry examine the substantive choices made by the state. The second question, therefore, is has the government, in pursuing its objectives, opted for the method that least impinges on rights. The third question is, has the government policy disproportionately affected particular groups of people? If, for example, the effects of the government's actions were felt almost exclusively on, say,

Aboriginal people or gays and lesbians, the court might find that the government's actions cannot be justified under section 1 of the Charter.

Section 1 of the Charter poses a fairly stringent obligation on Canadian governments to justify their actions. However, in recent years, the courts have modified the standard somewhat and made it much easier for the government to meet the threshold required by section 1. In particular, the courts appear to have developed a range of approaches. For example, in matters of criminal law, where there is a potential for incarceration, the courts tend to hold the government to a fairly strict standard. In policy areas that are more regulatory, such as social and economic policy, the courts have been far more willing to grant the government a degree of leeway and discretion.[38] In particular, the court may be less likely to demand that the least intrusive mechanism be chosen, so long as the government takes into account and makes a reasonable effort to minimize the rights impact of its actions.

Courts in different countries have taken different approaches to the question of how to consider the state's obligation to justify violations of rights. Under the *European Convention on Human Rights*, a proportionality standard similar to Canada's has developed. The United States constitution, however, has no provision similar to section 1 of the *Canadian Charter of Rights and Freedoms*. As a result, the courts have developed an approach to interpreting rights that builds into their very definition the possibility of their limitations. Consequently, different rights, depending on their constitutional significance, are subjected to different levels of scrutiny. Infringements on freedom of expression that limit political speech, for example, are subjected to what is known as "strict scrutiny," while infringements of commercial expression may be subjected to less vigorous analysis. The effect of this approach, however, is to somewhat ease the legal burden on the state to justify its actions, as the initial burden falls to applicants to demonstrate that their rights have been violated. It may require less to establish the violation depending on the type of case, but the burden remains with the applicants to prove a violation of their rights.

Appeals
If unsuccessful at trial, the applicant may want to appeal the court's decision. Of course, even if successful, the other side—the government or any other party to the action—can also appeal. This is a much more restrictive stage of the judicial process, both in terms of the opportunities for group members to participate in the process and the issues that can be considered. An appeal usually consists of a hearing before a panel of

judges. The number of judges will vary depending on the level of the court and the complexity of the issues. In provincial courts of appeal, panels are normally made up of three judges. All nine judges of the Supreme Court of Canada frequently sit to hear a case where constitutional issues are raised. Each participant presents a written submission, referred to as a "factum," which includes a summary of the issues and legal arguments being raised on the appeal. Usually an appeal does not challenge all aspects of the trial decision, so the factum narrows the issues and specifies to the judges just what is being contested. In addition to the written submissions, there is also an oral hearing where the parties have an opportunity to present their legal arguments to the appeal court. This is an opportunity both for the parties to directly address the court and for the judges to ask questions of the lawyers. The time allotted to oral arguments is often quite limited, which makes the written factums particularly important. No witnesses are called during an appeal, and new evidence is seldom presented. The only participants for the parties, therefore, are the lawyers.

It is a mistake to think that any issue raised at the trial can be challenged on appeal. Appeal courts usually only consider issues of law and will not examine findings of fact made by the trial judge. This means that if the trial judge rejects certain evidence or testimony as lacking in credibility, or expresses a preference for the testimony of one witness over another, such determinations cannot be challenged on appeal. The appeal proceeds based on the evidentiary/factual record as determined by the trial judge. The rationale for this limitation is that the trial judge hears the presentation of the evidence and, consequently, is in the best position to weigh conflicting evidence and assess the credibility of witnesses. The appeal court, on the other hand, has little on which to base such determinations other than the assurances of the lawyers appearing before it.

Consequently, a trial judge's finding of fact generally cannot be appealed. Only if the trial judge has made an error of law—that is, incorrectly applying the rules of evidence—can evidentiary findings be overturned. It also means, as indicated above, that new evidence is generally not permitted during an appeal. It is the parties' responsibility to ensure that all relevant evidence is presented during the trial stage of the process. Only in exceptional circumstances, where it would have been impossible for the evidence to have been presented at trial, will the court permit new evidence to be introduced at the appeal stage. This, however, is a very strict standard. It is not enough simply for the parties to demonstrate that they did not have the evidence, or were unaware of it.

If it was possible for them to have acquired the evidence or to have been aware of it, even if they did not or were not, then they will be prevented from introducing new evidence. It has to have been physically impossible in any circumstance for them to have had the evidence at trial for the appeal court to grant a motion for the introduction of new evidence at that stage.

The appeal court, then, considers legal issues. An appeal usually focuses on the trial judge's interpretation and application of the law to the issues raised by the case. The sorts of specific issues that are often the focus of an appeal include:

- the interpretation of legislation;
- the interpretation and application of precedents (past cases);
- the application of common law rules and principles;
- the application of rules of evidence; and
- in criminal cases, the judge's charge to the jury.

If an appeal is successful, there are several possible outcomes. The appeal court may simply substitute its decision for that of the trial court. If, for example, the appeal court decides the trial judge misinterpreted a statute, its judgement will indicate the correct way of interpreting the statute, apply it to the facts of the case and issue the appropriate remedy. In criminal cases the outcome is somewhat different. Where an appeal from a conviction is successful the court can issue an acquittal, but it is more common for a new trial to be ordered. This is often because the error that led to the appeal is either the incorrect application of a rule of evidence—leading to evidence to be either wrongly admitted or ex-cluded—or an error in the judge's charge to the jury. In both cases it can be difficult for the appeal court to predict what the outcome of the case would have been had the legal error not occurred in the first place.

The rules for appeals in criminal cases in Canada and the United States differ in important ways. In Canada, both the state and the accused have rights of appeal from the decision of the trial court. In the United States, only the accused has a right of appeal: a finding of not guilty means the absolute acquittal of the accused. There is no possibility of the state appealing that decision and trying the individual a second time. In Canada, however, the Crown has the right to appeal an acquittal and frequently does. There have been instances of individuals being tried a number of times on the same charge because of appeals.

The appeal is an important stage in the trial process. It provides an

The Euthanasia Debate in Canada

The question of whether or not the practice of euthanasia should be permitted, and under what conditions, has been the subject of a number of cases in Canada. In *R v. Rodriguez* [1993] 3 SCR 519, this issue was put directly before the court by Sue Rodriguez, who was suffering from ALS. Rodriguez sought a court declaration that provisions of the *Criminal Code* making it an offence to assist someone to commit suicide violated her rights under the *Canadian Charter of Rights and Freedoms*. The issue also came before the courts in *R v. Latimer* [2001] 1 S.C.R. 3. Latimer was convicted of second-degree murder in the death of his severely disabled daughter. He argued both that his actions were justified under the law of necessity and that his sentence of life imprisonment with no chance of parole for ten years constituted cruel and unusual punishment and violated the *Canadian Charter of Rights and Freedoms*. Groups on both sides of the euthanasia debate intervened in these cases to argue their views before the courts. Much of the argument, therefore, focused on the policy implications of euthanasia, which provided an important context for the court's interpretation of the *Criminal Code* in both cases.

excellent opportunity to develop the political and policy dimensions of the case. While the trial primarily deals with establishing the factual context for the case, on appeal, the judges are exclusively concerned with the issues of law. Consequently, policy arguments based on the potential ramifications of different interpretations of legislation, cases or constitutional provisions are given considerable attention by the judges. As a result, it is often at the appeal stage that other groups become involved as intervenors. Moreover, at the appellate court level, the judges have greater opportunity to carefully study the issues. The assistance of law clerks and a less onerous case load allow the judges to spend considerable time contemplating the issues before writing their judgements. Consequently, in complex cases it may be over a year before a final court of appeal issues its decision. Trial judges who labour with very heavy loads simply do not have the time and resources to consider their judgements so carefully. It is at the appeal stage, then, that political and policy issues become the focus of attention and may dominate the proceedings.

Notes

1. There are a number of good books that serve as introductions to the legal system. See, for example, Patrick Fitzgerald and Barry Wright, *Looking at Law: Canada's Legal System* (Toronto: Butterworths, 2000); S.M. Waddams, *Introduction to the Study of Law* (Scarborough: Carswell, 1997); Ian McLeod, *Legal Method* (London: MacMillan Press Ltd., 1996).
2. In some instances, depending on the nature of the remedy sought and the level of court where the action is commenced, a plaintiff may be referred to as an applicant and the defendant as a respondent. This is usually the case

where the remedy sought is a "declaration" as to the constitutional validity of governmental action or where the case involves an application for judicial review in an administrative law matter.

3. For a further discussion of the rules of intervention, see P. Muldoon, *The Law of Intervention: Status and Practice* (Aurora, Ont.: Canada Law Book, 1989).

4. *Andrews v. Law Society of British Columbia* [1989] 1 S.C.R. 143. Andrews was a British subject permanently resident in Canada. He was challenging provisions of the *Law Society Act* of British Columbia that required lawyers to be Canadian citizens. Andrews was a citizen of South Africa who had completed law school in British Columbia, articled and completed the bar admission course. He argued that his exclusion from practice constituted discrimination on the basis of national origin. This was an important case as it was the first consideration of the Charter's equality rights provisions by the Supreme Court of Canada.

5. In a recent criminal trial in Manitoba, the Canadian Police Association sought to intervene in a constitutional challenge to a *Criminal Code* provision that makes the slaying of a police officer a mandatory first-degree murder charge. The court denied intervenor status on the grounds that the association's position would be adequately represented by the Crown prosecutor. See Mike McIntyre, "Mountie-killing Case Begins: Police Furious Over Being Frozen Out of Challenge," *Winnipeg Free Press*, Feb. 26, 2003, p. A1.

6. The Women's Legal Education and Action Fund, for example, successfully sought intervenor status in the case of *Seaboyer & Gayme v. The Queen,* both at trial and on subsequent appeals. For a discussion of LEAF's role in these proceedings see Sherene Razack, *Canadian Feminism and the Law* (Toronto: Second Story Press, 1991), p. 55–57 and 109–20.

7. Gregory Hein, *Interest Group Litigation and Canadian Democracy* (Montreal: Institute for Research on Public Policy, 2000).

8. Ibid., p. 11–12.

9. It is important to remember that in many of these cases governments may also seek intervenor status. Consequently, where a constitutional challenge is brought to federal or provincial legislation, it is not uncommon for the Attorneys General from the other provinces to intervene in the case before the Supreme Court of Canada.

10. See below at page 96 for a further discussion of the costs of litigation.

11. For an interesting discussion of the selection of a plaintiff in a public interest case, see Doug Smith, *How to Tax a Billionaire*, (Winnipeg: Arbeiter Ring Publishing, 2002), ch. 5.

12. See *Tremblay v. Daigle* [1989] 2 S.C.R. 530 for a good example of a case in which there was little choice with respect to individual involved in the litigation. In this instance, Chantal Daigle's ex-boyfriend, Jean-Guy Tremblay, had sought an injunction to prevent Daigle from having an abortion. Daigle was supported by the Canadian Abortion Rights Action League in defending

herself against the injunction application. After the Supreme Court ruled against Tremblay it was revealed that Daigle had already had the procedure. Subsequently, Daigle joined the anti-abortion movement and actively campaigned against abortion rights.

13. See, for example, *Gouriet v. Union of Post Office Workers* [1978] AC 435 (Eng. H.L).

14. Although it should be noted that in the United Kingdom the Attorney General is not a member of cabinet.

15. Gouriet, supra. note 13.

16. *Valley Forge Christian College v. Americans United for Separation of Church and State, Inc.,* 454 U.S. 464 (1982)

17. *Thorson v. Attorney General of Canada* [1975] 1 S.C.R. 138; *Nova Scotia Board of Censors v. McNeil* [1976] 2 S.C.R. 265; and *Minister of Justice of Canada v. Borowski* [1981] 2 S.C.R. 575.

18. See the review of common law standing rules in *The Canadian Council of Churches v. The Queen* [1992] 1 S.C.R. 236, p. 243–48.

19. Ibid, p. 253–54.

20. Doug Smith, *How to Tax a Billionaire*, supra. note 11.

21. *Canadian Council of Churches*, supra. note 18.

22. *Finlay v. Canada (Minister of Finance)* [1986] 2 S.C.R. 607.

23. Court Challenges Program, <www.www.ccppcj.ca>.

24. On the difficulties faced by APEC protesters in financing their appearances before the RCMP Public Complaints Commission, see Karen Busby, "Raising the Dough: Funding for Lawyers at Public Inquiries," in Wesley Pue, (ed.) *Pepper in our Eyes, The APEC Affair* (Vancouver: UBC Press, 2000), p. 171–84. Busby makes the point that virtually all participants except the student demonstrators had their lawyers paid for out of the public purse.

25. For example, Mary Eberts, a prominent human rights lawyer in Toronto, was ordered to stop representing the Native Women's Association of Canada in its efforts to stop a referendum on the ratification of the Charlottetown Constitutional Accord. Other prominent members of Eberts' firm had supported the Accord. Eberts eventually took a leave of absence from the firm and continued representing the association, without the resources of the firm available to her. See "Law Firm Courted Controversy by Refusing Case," *Vancouver Sun*, Nov. 30, 1992, p. A6.

26. The crisis in legal aid has led the Canadian Bar Association to contemplate suing the government to increase funding to legal aid programs, and to many lawyers withdrawing their services. See Janice Tibbetts, "Lawyers Hope to make Legal Aid a Charter Right," *National Post*, March 7, 2002, p. A9. For an overview of legal aid in Canada, see National Council of Welfare, *Legal Aid and the Poor* (Ottawa: National Council of Welfare, 1995).

27. For a listing, see Legal Aid Ontario's Web site at <www.legalaid.on.ca/en/specialty.asp>. On the services provided by legal aid clinics in Ontario, see Vera Chouinard, "Challenging Law's Empire: Rebellion, Incorporation,

and Changing Geographics of Power in Ontario's Legal Clinic System," *Studies in Political Economy* 55 (1988) p. 65–92 and Byron Sheldrick, "Law, Representation, and Political Activism: Community Based Practice and the Mobilization of Legal Resources" (1995) *Canadian Journal of Law and Society* 10, p. 155–84.

28. Details are available from the Court Challenges Program Web site, <www.www.ccppcj.ca>.
29. Lara Friedlander, "Costs and the Public Interest Litigant" *McGill Law Journal* 40 (1995), p. 55, 61.
30. Ibid, p. 66.
31. See Ontario Rules of Civil Procedure, Rule 56.01.
32. See Lara Friedlander, "Costs and the Public Interest Litigant," supra. note 29 for a discussion of the case of *Kennett v. Health Sciences Centre* (1991) 76 Man. R. (2d) 47. In that case a family of Jehovah's Witnesses were challenging the constitutionality of the Manitoba *Child and Family Services Act*, which allowed the hospital to provide their child with a blood transfusion over their objections. The family, which was not resident in Manitoba, was ordered to pay $46,000 in security for costs.
33. Ontario was the last province in Canada to permit contingency fees, with amendments to the *Solicitors Act* passed in December 2002.
34. *Halpern et al v. Attorney General of Ontario* (June 10, 2003) Ontario Court of Appeal # C39172;C39174, available at <www.canlii.org/on/cas/onca/2003/2003onca10314.html>.
35. See Court Challenges Program, <www.www.ccppcj.ca>.
36. For a discussion of the APEC protests and the RCMP Public Complaints Commission, see Wes Pue, *Pepper in our Eyes,* supra. note 24. The Report of the RCMP Public Complaints Commission is available from the Commission and can be found at <www.cpc-cpp.gc.ca/ePub/APEC/eFinalApec.pdf>.
37. In criminal cases the onus of proof rests on the prosecution to prove all elements of the offence.
38. See Janet Hiebert, *Limiting Rights: The Dilemma of Judicial Review* (Montreal: McGill-Queen's University Press, 1996).

Chapter 6

The Administrative State

When we consider the potential of engaging law as part of a political struggle, we generally think of courts as the vehicle by which this might be achieved. To a certain extent, this reflects the legacy of American public interest litigation, which pioneered the use of test cases to advance and assert the constitutional rights of disadvantaged groups. The focus on courts, however, ignores the existence of other judicial and quasi-judicial arenas that social action groups might find useful as a political resource. In particular, the expansion of the welfare state in the post-World War II era included the creation of regulatory and administrative bodies, many of which operate on a quasi-judicial framework. These agencies engage in a wide range of tasks, including policymaking and adjudication, and operate in a host of policy contexts. Some work within the social welfare field, regulating access to social assistance and other benefits of the welfare state, while others operate within the economic field, regulating everything from collective bargaining to the operation of the stock market. Still others perform a disciplinary function, overseeing the performance of the police, lawyers, doctors and other professional groups.

Administrative boards and tribunals operate within such a broad range of policy contexts that it is difficult to generalize. Many can set their own procedures and organizational structures. Each board develops its own jurisprudence and its own specialized expertise. This diversity speaks to the development of a pluralistic legal order. While the courts strive to achieve a coherent and consistent body of law, a number of different legal systems exist within the state. Social assistance law is different from securities law, which is different in turn from the practice of environmental appeal boards. What is common to each, however, is the need to hold hearings that replicate a judicial process. Consequently, these boards and tribunals may provide opportunities for social action groups to attain representation within the policymaking structures of the state itself, at an earlier and more useful stage than is generally achieved by going to court.

A Brief History of the Regulatory Boards

As suggested, the growth of administrative boards and tribunals paralleled the growth of the welfare state. After World War II, western governments were eager to avoid a return to the conditions of economic crisis that had characterized the Great Depression. The dominant policy paradigm that emerged during this period came to be called Keynesianism, in which governments assume an important role in regulating the economy. In particular, by utilizing the state's regulatory and spending power, the demand for goods in the economy could be managed and the "boom or bust" tendencies of capitalist economies smoothed out.[1]

The groundwork for the increased regulatory role of the state had been laid during World War II, when governments ran the economy as part of the war effort. This increased state presence in regulating economic activity continued as part of the Keynesian policy mix. In addition, state spending on infrastructure developments, such as roads, utilities, hospitals and schools, also increased during this period. The state also designed a range of new social programs to ensure that people were not too adversely affected by economic downturns. Social security, unemployment insurance, old age pensions, disability benefits and medicare were all post-war developments that sought to ensure that the temporarily or permanently unemployed did not become destitute. They also ensured that these individuals continued to contribute to the economy through the buying power provided by their social welfare benefits. Both policy directions were effectively designed to increase demand in the economy. In the economic field, this was achieved by direct state spending on projects that produced employment, either in the construction field or in the expansion of the public sector itself. In the social field, it was achieved through benefits that ensured people still had money to spend on goods and services.

Both policy directions, however, required a level of state regulation that had not existed up to that point. It also required the development of new administrative mechanisms and vehicles. Regulatory boards and tribunals filled this need. In the economic area, new administrative bodies were established to regulate particular sectors of the economy to ensure orderly growth and development. The Canadian Transportation Commission, for example, played an important role in regulating the growth of the country's transportation network, particularly the emerging airline industry. The National Energy Board played a similar role in the vital energy sector, while the Canadian Radio-television and Telecommunications Commission (CRTC) regulated the growth and expansion of Canadian broadcasting.

The post-war period was also characterized by the utilization of crown corporations as policy vehicles. In the case of public utilities, such as electricity and water, administrative boards were given responsibility for regulating their operation and, particularly, the mandate to oversee their setting of rates. Other boards were established to regulate areas of the economy that raised particular problems. Labour relations tribunals, for example, regulated collective bargaining and strikes to ensure labour peace. Environmental assessment boards, on the other hand, were established to ensure that the environmental impacts of development were not too great, while permitting development to proceed in an orderly fashion.

In the social sphere, a wide range of administrative boards were also created. Social welfare programs operated to insulate and cushion people from market forces. Consequently, access to these programs is often strictly regulated.[2] Unemployment insurance commissions, welfare benefits appeal boards, workers' compensation commissions, refugee and immigration boards and rent review tribunals are examples of administrative boards that operate in the social policy area. Their role is both to ensure that people entitled to benefits do receive them, but also that access to the programs is carefully monitored and controlled. In many instances these agencies sit as an appeal body for the decisions of front-line bureaucrats.

Structure of Administrative Boards and Tribunals

Administrative boards take on a number of different forms and operate in a wide range of contexts. The specific powers and responsibilities of each are found in its particular mandating or "enabling" legislation. The legislation that created the agency will set out its powers and responsibilities, as well as the process to be followed in carrying out that mandate. There is considerable variation, however, in how specific the enabling legislation is. In some instances, it defines the jurisdiction of a board in quite specific, narrow terms. In other instances, it provides a broad mandate to the board with very little guidance. Procedurally, most boards have considerable discretion as to how they organize and conduct their affairs, although again this can vary from context to context.

Administrative boards fulfil a number of roles. They provide an investigatory/regulatory and policy development function, which is frequently combined with an adjudicative function. Many boards adjudicate and decide individual and specific cases. The CRTC, for example, reviews licence applications and determines with what terms and conditions a broadcaster is required to comply.[3] The board sometimes has to adjudicate between competing applications. In performing this adjudicative function, however, the board is also clearly regulating the broadcasting industry and developing policy. In this respect, the CRTC has played an important role in determining Canadian content rules, access to local community programming on cable services, and the presence of specialized programming geared to particular cultural communities. In other words, the CRTC plays a significant role in determining the policies that govern broadcasting in the country.

The particular mix of regulatory, policy and adjudicative functions varies from tribunal to tribunal. While the CRTC, for example, has a broad policy mandate, other boards have a more limited jurisdiction that emphasizes the adjudication of specific disputes. Welfare appeal boards, for example, tend to have a limited policy role. Their mandate is to ensure that decisions regarding welfare entitlements have been made in accordance with the requirements of the legislation. This may involve a fairly mechanical application of formulae set out in the legislation.[4] It would be very wrong, however, to assume that such boards have no policy role. Enabling legislation is frequently vague and uncertain, and this gives boards some discretion in shaping its application. Although the policy mandate of some boards may not be explicit, most have the capacity to shape policy to some extent. Welfare appeal boards, for example, confront ambiguities in social assistance legislation that require choosing between competing interpretations and understandings of poverty issues.

Boards and tribunals offer several advantages for social action groups seeking to influence policy. One of the rationales for the creation of administrative boards is the need, given the complexity of state regulation, to bring expertise to the adjudication of disputes. Courts can be criticized for lacking the policy expertise to adequately consider many of the issues brought before them. Administrative boards and tribunals, on the other hand, frequently have considerable and specialized expertise. While judges tend to be generalists, those who staff administrative boards tend to be specialists. Members of a labour board, therefore, will likely have a background in labour relations, while panel members of an environmental review board will be knowledgeable in environmental issues.

While one of the advantages of administrative boards may be expertise, it should not be assumed that all boards possess that expertise. There are frequently no criteria for the appointment of individuals to regulatory boards and tribunals. In some instances these appointments can be used as a patronage tool by governments. An environmental regulatory board will be of less use to environmental groups if the government has appointed to it only pro-development individuals. At the same time, given that all new development projects require the regulatory approval of the board, environmental groups cannot afford to ignore it. In these cases, the appointment of board members may become a political issue that the groups choose to emphasize.

One of the safeguards built into the judicial system is the concept of an independent judiciary. Judges are supposed to operate and make their decisions outside of the political process. For this reason, political interference or attempts to influence a judge are impermissible and will generally require the resignation/dismissal of the politician involved. At the same time, judges have security of tenure and cannot be dismissed from their positions without cause. While judicial independence does not apply to administrative tribunals in quite the same way, a similar concept does exist. One of the rationales for creating administrative boards was to remove controversial and/or difficult issues from the political arena. In this way, individuals feel they have been treated fairly and that decisions regarding the allocation of resources and the distribution of benefits have not been politically manipulated.

For this reason, regulatory agencies operate at "arms length" from the politicians. While the labour board, for example, might formally fall under the jurisdiction of the minister of labour, it operates independently from the minister. It would, therefore, be viewed as highly inappropriate for the minister to interfere with the operation of the board. For this reason, however, while the minister might be able to appoint whomever she pleases, appointments clearly designed to politicize the board would become a political issue.

In addition to the expertise of panel members, regulatory boards and tribunals have a number of structural advantages over courts that permit them to play a more effective policy role. Many administrative boards have their own staff, which provide research and policy development support. For example, human rights commissions conduct research and report on particular human rights issues, and play a public education function in addition to adjudicating individual cases. Another example is Canada's National Energy Board, which has a staff of approximately 280, including financial analysts, computer specialists, economists, engineers, environmentalists, geologists, geophysicists, lawyers and library specialists.[5] With the exception of appellate courts, where judges may have the services of law clerks, most courts lack an independent research capacity.

The structure of some boards is explicitly designed to permit broader representation of interests and perspectives during the hearing of specific cases. Labour boards in Canada, for example, utilize a tripartite structure in which each panel comprises a chairperson and two "side persons" or nominees, one chosen from a union background and the other from a management background.[6] Assuming that the union and management nominees will usually vote for their sides, this leaves the real decision-making power with the chairperson of the panel. The presence of the nominees, however, ensures that union and management perspectives are actively represented in the decision-making process. It recognizes that the decision of the board is not purely adjudicative, but also has a policy context.

In other instances structures are in place to ensure that arguments not advanced by the parties are put nonetheless before the board. Some boards, for example, have their own counsel whose job is to put those arguments before the board that have been overlooked or that it feels are in the public interest. This structure is frequently used in commissions of inquiry, where commission counsel takes the lead in presenting evidence before the hearings. In these instances, which constitute a marked departure from the adversarial system, it is assumed that the public interest demands an independent presentation of all relevant evidence, rather than a reliance on interested parties who will only present evidence that is beneficial to their case. Other administrative and regulatory boards also use this structure, as do securities commissions, which regulate the operation of the stock market, and the National Energy Board.

Commission counsel are generally assumed to be non-adversarial. In other words, they do not necessarily take a position supporting or opposing any of the parties before the board. Their role is to assist both the board and the parties before it. It would be incorrect, however, to assume that all commission counsel operate in this fashion. Frequently they take an adversarial position or, at the very least, have a particular policy perspective they wish to advance.

Nevertheless, the presence of commission counsel can be particularly important where parties have no legal representation. The Immigration and Refugee Board, for example, employs refugee hearings officers (RHOs). The responsibility of an RHO is to provide the board with the information it requires to determine whether a refugee claimant meets the definition of a refugee under the *United Nations Convention on Refugees*.[7] Individual claimants appear before the board and tell their stories as to why they fled their homes. Often, individuals are unrepresented. There is, in this administrative structure, no one who actively opposes the refugee

Funding Intervenors at Administrative Hearings

In Manitoba, the Public Utilities Board oversees utility and auto insurance rates. Under Manitoba legislation, the costs of Public Utilities Board hearings and the costs of intervenor participation are charged back to the utilities. This represents a significant cost to the users, but ensures widespread representation of interests in the regulatory process.

claimant. The RHO may oppose an application where the evidence indicates the claim does not fall within the Convention definition. At the same time, however, the RHO may support an application and indeed bring before the board information and material in support of a claim that the individual applicant would not otherwise have access to.

This raises an important point. The rules of procedure are frequently less rigid in administrative boards and tribunals than they are in courts. This makes them more accessible to individuals and groups than the courts. This flexibility is evident in a number of different ways.

The normal rules of evidence are generally not applied in administrative tribunals. The rules are much more flexible and adaptable. Consequently, it is easier for individuals and groups to operate within the administrative environment without the aid of a lawyer. Administrative boards are also generally not bound by the normal rules of precedent that govern the common law courts. It is much easier for an administrative board to simply make a decision based on the merits of the particular case without reference to past board decisions. Having said this, administrative tribunals often develop their own concept of precedent simply to provide a mechanism for ensuring consistency in decision-making. Finally, administrative boards do not make orders for costs. All parties are responsible for their own costs of participation, although some may have state support.

Intervention may also be an easier process, particularly where state financial support is available. Many boards take the position that parties before it should have a direct interest in the hearings.[8] However, they also acknowledge the importance of public interest groups and the valuable contribution they can make. Some boards will be more open to intervenors than others. Generally, the greater the policy role of the board, the greater the likelihood that fairly liberal intervention rules will be applied.

Moreover, while lawyers are not necessary for representation before an administrative board, in many instances it may be desirable to have one. Administrative law has become a highly specialized area of the profession, and some lawyers concentrate on appearing before particular tribunals. While rules of procedure may be more flexible than in courts, it is also true that the regular appearance of lawyers before boards and tribunals has had the effect of judicializing their processes and making them increasingly court-like in appearance and process.

Nevertheless, it is easier for individuals to represent themselves before an administrative board, and there are a number of agents and non-lawyers who regularly appear before administrative agencies. Union grievance officers, for example, who often are not lawyers, frequently appear before labour boards. Community activists who have developed an expertise in welfare rights law regularly appear before boards with a social welfare mandate.[9]

The existence of these resources within the community makes it less expensive for groups to appear before tribunals. Indeed, one of the advantages of boards and tribunals is that they do provide a relatively inexpensive mechanism for adjudicating cases compared to the courts. It may, therefore, be possible for a social action group to become an effective "repeat player" in the administrative environment. The National Anti-Poverty Organization has targeted administrative boards whose decisions have an impact on the poor. It has, for example, regularly appeared before the CRTC to oppose increases in rates for basic telephone services.

It would be a mistake, however, to assume that resources do not matter in the administrative context. Hearings in complex cases can extend for months and even years. Environmental review board hearings into a proposed landfill site near Smithville in Southern Ontario lasted for over ten years. In the end, the development was turned down by the board, a clear victory for opponents of the development. Nevertheless, the cost of such an endeavour can be very high. Also, because of the technical and specialized nature of many administrative boards, there may be a greater need for expert witnesses and preparation of specialized research and reports.

A lack of professional legal representation or the incapacity to hire experts may be a very serious impediment to a group appearing before a regulatory board. In 1986 the Ontario Municipal Board considered a proposed amendment to the City of Toronto's official development plan. The amendment would have permitted development of the so-called railway lands on Toronto's lakeshore. In particular, the amendment was required to permit construction of the Toronto Skydome, home to the Toronto Blue Jays. At the hearings into the proposed amendment, every property owner in the area was represented, frequently by both lawyers and urban planners hired as experts. Many of these parties did not play an active role in the hearing, but rather were there simply to monitor the proceedings and safeguard their clients' interests in the future development of the land.

Only two groups opposed the development. One was a coalition of local groups led by Jack Layton, then a Toronto City Councillor. Mr. Layton cross-examined witnesses on behalf of the group, which did not have legal representation. Given Mr. Layton's other responsibilities at city hall, the group's participation in the hearings was sporadic. The other group was a local ratepayers association. While initially represented by a lawyer, the hearing dragged on for several months and eventually the group could no longer afford its lawyer. The president of the group, who had no legal training, took over representing the association. While he did an admirable job, he was unable to effectively question witnesses. His group did not have the resources to counter the overwhelming support for the development that had been mustered in the hearing room. In the end, the plan amendment was approved with virtually no changes.

It is possible, however, for groups with particular expertise and knowledge to become important repeat players within the administrative context. The Canadian Environmental Law Association (CELA), for example, is a specialized legal clinic devoted to environmental issues. It plays an important role in representing individuals and groups both in the courts and before administrative boards. It is also involved in public education, lobbying and law reform, and serves as an important resource for environmental groups.[10] In many respects, CELA is more than simply a legal clinic: it has become a social movement organization unto itself, with close connections to a range of environmental organizations and movements. Organizations like CELA become important participants in the environmental policy community and the existence of administrative boards and tribunals provides them with a vehicle by which their participation can have an impact on environmental law.

In other instances, participation before an administrative tribunal may be a "one-off" event for a group. The hearings of the RCMP Public Complaints Commission into the conduct of the RCMP at the APEC meetings in Vancouver in 1997 is a good example. In that instance individuals and groups brought complaints to the Commission alleging RCMP mistreatment, through the use of pepper spray and the arrest of demonstrators. They also alleged that the Prime Minister's office had directed the RCMP to prevent demonstrators from getting close to President Suharto of Indonesia. In this instance, although the demonstrators might have preferred some other vehicle for advancing their political message, the administrative structure dictated that these cases go to the

Public Complaints Commission. The lengthy hearings provided a forum for the demonstrators' anti-globalization and human rights messages, as well as a spotlight under which the groups attempted to demonstrate a connection between the Prime Minister and his political staff and the suppression of dissent. The Commission proceedings did not provide a completely satisfactory vehicle for exposing these links. Nevertheless, the groups involved got considerable political mileage out of the hearings and the Commission's final report was a vindication for the demonstrators.

Administrative tribunals have created an alternative legal structure to that of the courts. Moreover, given the alternative and flexible structures employed by administrative boards and tribunals, they provide a relatively inexpensive and accessible vehicle by which groups can insert themselves into the policy process. An important limitation of administrative tribunals is the fact that many of them are relatively obscure, and their hearings rarely garner the sort of media attention that a court case does. In the administrative context, many of the same concerns discussed in Chapter 5 also apply. While boards may be more flexible and informal than courts, they still operate within a judicial or quasi-judicial framework. Lawyers, while not essential, still dominate proceedings in many administrative tribunals. Hiring expert witnesses or having technical reports prepared remains an expensive proposition. Groups can more easily become repeat players, although this may make it more difficult to pursue a broader political agenda. In short, the same sorts of cautions discussed in Chapter 5 must also be reiterated here. Judicial strategies tend to be most effective when integrated into a broader political agenda, rather than being the group's sole *raison d'être*. In that context, the group needs to maintain control over its agenda and participate only when it is beneficial to do so.

Judicial Review of Administrative Decisions: The Courts and Administrative Boards

Administrative boards and tribunals constitute a policy-specific legal order. Each board has its own rules and structure. This does not mean, however, that the courts play no role in the administrative context. Indeed, those who are unhappy with the decisions of administrative bodies may try to overturn them by recourse to the courts. While it is possible to have an administrative decision overturned by the courts, it is difficult. At one time, courts were quite willing to substitute their preferences for the decisions of administrative boards. Over time, however, courts have moved toward respecting the autonomy of boards and their decision-making expertise. Consequently, courts are generally loath to interfere with the decisions of administrative boards and tribunals.

This reluctance of courts to interfere with boards is a double-edged sword. Whether it is a good thing or not depends on how one assesses the decisions of a particular board. On the one hand, judicial reticence to intervene preserves the policymaking integrity of the board and prevents individuals and groups dissatisfied with specific decisions from stepping outside the process in pursuit of a different outcome. On the other hand, in some instances, such reticence leaves adverse decisions intact.

The question of whether or not one may go to court to overturn an administrative decision raises a very complex area of administrative law. There are a number of different routes that might be taken to challenge decisions of the state. Where the decision involves constitutional rights, such as a violation of the *Canadian Charter of Rights and Freedoms*, then an application may be made directly to the courts. In the absence of a constitutional right, however, the mechanism for seeking judicial re-course depends on the enabling statute of the administrative board and/ or the nature of the specific claim.

Depending on what the enabling legislation provides, decisions of administrative bodies may be challenged either through an appeal or judicial review. Of these two, an appeal provides a broader basis of challenge because the reviewing court is entitled to reconsider the board's or tribunal's decision and, if it disagrees, substitute its own. It is important to remember, however, that appeals are generally granted only on questions of law and not on questions of fact. What this means is that the court will consider the legal reasoning employed by the board in reaching its decision, including how it interpreted any statutory provi-sions or other legal rules, but it will not reconsider any findings of fact by the board.

The board's enabling legislation will determine whether there exists a right of appeal from an administrative board or tribunal. If there is a right to appeal to the courts, the legislation creating the board will stipulate this. It will also set out to whom the appeal is to be made. In most instances this will be a court, but it may also be to another administrative body. Appeals from the Ontario Workers' Compensation Board, for example, are to the Workers' Compensation Appeal Board. Appeals from municipal welfare determinations may be to a social assistance review board. In other instances, a decision from a board may be appealed to what in most instances would be considered a political entity. The decisions of some administrative boards can be appealed to cabinet. National Energy Board decisions, for example, are normally appealed to the Federal Court of Canada, but there can be an additional appeal to the federal cabinet. In most instances, however, appeals are taken to a court. Decisions of federal administrative boards and tribunals are appealed to the Federal Court, while provincial boards and tribunal decisions are appealed to the appropriate level of the provincial court system.

In many instances the enabling legislation of a board or tribunal does not provide for an appeal, but this does not mean their decisions are beyond review in the courts. It does mean, however, that the challenge must be by way of the more limited grounds of judicial review, rather than by way of a full appeal. Judicial review is a specialized doctrine of administrative law that permits the courts to oversee administrative decisions to ensure they accord with the law.

In its modern form, judicial review owes much to A.V. Dicey, a British constitutional theorist who wrote during the late nineteenth century.[11] Dicey was writing very much within a classical liberal frame-work. He opposed the expansion of the state, which he saw as evidence of "collectivist" tendencies that threatened individual liberty and free-dom. The expansion of the state's administrative capacity brought with it increased discretion on the part of state officials and the possibility of capricious and arbitrary decisions. For Dicey, law was a mechanism for containing the growth of the state and safeguarding against arbitrary political decisions. The rule of law aided this by requiring all state actions to be legally mandated. This was achieved by a series of interrelated concepts that comprise the modern doctrine of the rule of law. First, an individual cannot be punished or penalized for her actions unless they are prohibited by law. Second, in the absence of a legal grant of power, state officials have no greater authority than ordinary citizens. And third, the ordinary courts of the land, rather than administrative bodies, are consti-tutionally authorized to safeguard and protect individual rights. Dicey viewed this final element of the rule of law as particularly important for protecting individual property rights through the common law.

The legal doctrine of judicial review is based on this vision of the rule of law. Its primary purpose is to ensure that administrative decisions have a proper legal foundation. Enabling legislation draws boundaries around the administrative board or tribunal that defines its authority. The courts, through judicial review, are concerned with ensuring that the decision-maker stays within these boundaries and does not stray beyond the scope of legal authority granted it. This necessitates a different sort of analysis on the part of the courts than takes place on an appeal. In theory, the courts are concerned less with the substantive decision reached by the board and more with how the decision was reached. This is reflected in the three primary grounds of judicial review: procedural irregularity, error of law and jurisdictional error.

Procedural irregularity requires that the board utilize a fair process in coming to its decisions. Some enabling statutes stipulate the process the board must follow, but in many instances the statute is silent on the issue or authorizes the board to establish its own procedures. Courts have always held that administrative procedure can be reviewed to ensure its fairness. While the requirements for a "fair process" have changed over time, the modern doctrine requires that decision-makers be unbiased and that those affected by a decision be given the opportunity both to know the case they must meet and to respond to it. In other words, individuals need to have access to the information upon which the decision is based, knowledge of the evidence considered and an opportunity to put their case forward to the decision-maker.

If the court concludes that a procedural error has been committed, it will "quash" the decision. This does not mean the decision is thereby reversed or overturned. Rather, it is nullified and the case is sent back to the original administrative board for a new decision. In effect, the board will fix the procedural error and issue a new decision. There is no prohibition, in a case of this sort, against the board coming to the same decision it reached the first time. For social action groups seeking to challenge administrative decisions, this is a significant limitation. Even if one is successful on a judicial review application, there is no guarantee of a different substantive outcome. The remedies available on judicial review, therefore, are significantly more limited than in a right of appeal.

Error of law and jurisdictional error are interconnected as grounds of review. Error of law requires that the decision-makers, in coming to their decision, correctly interpret the enabling legislation and any other general laws they need to consider in their deliberations. Jurisdictional error, on the other hand, simply requires that the board stay within the specific legislative jurisdiction granted to it.

Error of law provides the broadest scope for the court to effectively "reverse" the decision of an administrative board. By indicating to the board it it incorrectly interpreted the law, and what the correct interpretation should be, courts can effectively turn a judicial review into a de facto appeal. Historically, courts quite actively utilized error of law to substitute their preferred outcomes for the substantive decisions of administrative boards. This was particularly true in the field of labour law, where labour board decisions that expanded union rights were frequently overturned.[12]

The state moved to protect the integrity of its regulatory systems by introducing into enabling legislation special provisions called "privative clauses" or "ouster clauses." These clauses are designed to insulate administrative boards from judicial review. While the exact formulation of these clauses varies, they generally provide that the decisions of a board are "final and binding" and not subject to review by any court. Effectively, this means that decisions of the board cannot be reviewed for error of law, although it is still possible to review them for both procedural and jurisdictional errors. The rationale for the latter is that the courts assume privative clauses apply only to decisions that the board was authorized to make. These clauses do not prevent the court from ensuring that the board has stayed within the scope of its legal authority.

Historically, courts tended to get around privative clauses by simply reclassifying what would otherwise be considered an error of law into a jurisdictional question. In other words, they would deem a particular issue critical to the board's jurisdiction and if the board erred on that issue, it would "lose jurisdiction" and its decision would be susceptible to judicial oversight. In the landmark British case of *Anisminic Ltd. v. Foreign Compensation Commission*, the House of Lords went so far as to say that any error of law could be classified as jurisdictional, thereby preserving the court's right to oversee administrative boards, but also making privative clauses virtually meaningless.[13]

Over the past several decades, courts in Canada, Britain and the United States have all moved to a more functional approach to judicial review. Effectively, this means that the courts have come to acknowledge the importance of administration and moved away from the fundamentally hostile position reflected in the classical Diceyan approach. In Canada, the courts are now much more attentive to the existence of a privative clause and willing to defer to the expertise of the administrative board. The Canadian position is that courts should be very reluctant, in the face of a privative clause, to interfere with board decisions. They should only intervene when it can be said that a decision is "patently unreasonable."[14] Although what this means is not completely clear in all circumstances, it does set a fairly high threshold for judicial intervention. That the judge would have come to a different conclusion on the substantive questions raised by the case is an insufficient ground for the court to interfere.

More recently, Canadian courts have applied this deferential approach even to cases where there is no privative clause and there exists a right of appeal.[15] Increasingly the courts determine the appropriate standard of review to be applied to administrative boards on the basis of the administrative function and the degree of specialized expertise possessed. In effect, the greater the policy content of a board's mandate and the greater the expertise of the board, the more likely the courts will respect the board's decision-making process. On the other hand, where a board possesses no specialized expertise, and its enabling legislation does not appear to grant the board a policy role, the courts will feel more comfortable intervening.

The effect of these jurisprudential developments is to severely limit the potential of judicial review to challenge administrative decision-making. While administrative boards and tribunals may be important institutions through which social action groups seek to challenge and influence state policy, there is limited opportunity to step outside that process and utilize the courts to overturn negative board decisions. This is further compounded by the limited range of remedies available in a judicial review case. As discussed above, the normal remedy is for the court to simply quash the decision and send it back to the board for a rehearing. Even if successful, therefore, a victory in a judicial review case could turn out to be little more than symbolic if the board comes to the same decision on rehearing.

Municipalities and Judicial Review

Many decisions of concern to social action groups are made by municipal governments. This raises the issue of the degree to which the courts may be used to challenge decisions of the local state. Housing issues, local planning issues, local environmental and health issues, and the administration of welfare benefits may all fall within the jurisdiction of local government. Municipal governments frequently make important decisions regarding whether resources will be devoted to urban renewal and environmental projects, housing shelters and services for street people on the one hand, or infrastructure developments, corporate services and business tax rebates on the other.

Municipalities occupy an unusual position within the constitutional structure of most countries. In one sense, they are a democratically elected level of government with a range of legislative authority and taxation powers. Despite the significance of the powers exercised by municipalities, however, many municipal structures have no constitutional status of their own. The power and jurisdiction exercised by municipal governments is usually delegated to them by another level of government. In

Canada, for example, provincial governments create municipalities, while in the United Kingdom they are created by the central government. This means that municipalities only possess those specific powers granted to them by legislation, and their jurisdictional authority may be altered or amended at any time by the government that created them.[16] This situation was revealed in the late 1970s when the left-wing Greater London Council was disbanded by the neo-conservative government of Margaret Thatcher.[17] Although local borough councils continued to exist, London was without a municipal government structure until Tony Blair's Labour Government re-established one in 1999.

To a certain extent, then, municipalities have more in common with regulatory boards and tribunals than with legislatures. Despite their democratic trappings, the courts apply the same rules of administrative law to the decisions and deliberations of municipal governments as they do to any other administrative body. This means that the capacity to challenge city hall in the courts is subject to many of the limitations of administrative judicial review. The main basis for such challenges must rest on the principles of procedural fairness and jurisdiction. In other words, it is necessary to demonstrate that the local government either failed to follow its procedural rules in coming to a decision or that it went beyond the power granted to it in its enabling legislation.

Nevertheless, the courts do recognize that the democratic character of municipalities distinguishes them from other regulatory agencies. Municipalities, the courts have said, exercise a dual legislative and regulatory function. If anything, however, this recognition is employed in a highly contradictory and inconsistent fashion. In some instances the courts favour the municipal legislative function and turn a blind eye to improprieties that would lead to the quashing of decisions by most administrative bodies. In other instances, however, the courts apply the rules of administrative law strictly and invalidate decisions that they feel go beyond the proper scope of municipal decision-making.

The latter tendency is clearly illustrated by the 1994 decision of the Supreme Court of Canada in *Shell Canada Products v. The City of Vancouver*.[18] The City of Vancouver, in support of the campaign to end apartheid in South African, had passed a resolution to boycott Shell Canada products until it divested its interests in South Africa. Shell sought judicial review of the decision, arguing that the boycott went beyond the municipality's legislative jurisdiction. In particular, the *City of Vancouver Act* contained a provision that the city's legislative authority was to be exercised for the "good rule and government of the city." Shell argued, and the majority of the Supreme Court judiciary agreed, that boycotting Shell because of the political situation in another country had no connection to the governance of the city. Moreover, the Supreme Court went on to say that while purchasing decisions were properly within the mandate of the city government, the choice of supplier should be based on financial considerations of price and service. For the court, this was the only conceivable way of making a decision consistent with the city's jurisdiction and mandate. Discrimination between suppliers for commercial or business reasons was acceptable, but discrimination for non-business, non-commercial reasons was not.[19] In effect, the court removed from the city its purchasing power for non-commercial objectives.

In *Shell* the court refused to recognize the political and elected nature of the municipal government. Instead, it treated the municipality much as it would any administrative board that had exceeded its legislative mandate. The dissenting judges in the *Shell* case took a very different approach, arguing that the interpretation of the city's jurisdiction needed to take into account the political and legislative functions of municipal governments. In particular, they argued that the city's own interpretation of the "best interests" or well-being of the citizens of Vancouver should be treated with a certain amount of respect and deference. In light of the unique nature of municipalities, the dissenting judges argued that the courts should be reluctant to overturn any decision with a clearly political basis.[20]

Shell, then, is an example of the courts refusing to treat a municipality differently than other administrative bodies. The result ensured that big business would not be adversely affected by municipal politics. A different approach, but a similar result, can be seen in the recent decisions of the Manitoba courts in the Save the Eaton's Building Coalition cases. These cases involved a decision by the City of Winnipeg (with the support and agreement of both the provincial and federal governments) to permit the demolition of the historic downtown Eaton's building and the construction of a new hockey arena in its place.[21] When Eaton's declared bankruptcy in 1999, the store was left vacant. The City of Winnipeg has long struggled with the problem of redeveloping the downtown, which has a large number of empty buildings. When a prominent local capitalist proposed redeveloping the site and constructing a downtown arena, local politicians felt that a solution to the problem had been presented to them. The Eaton's site would not remain empty, and the new arena would serve as the focal point for the downtown redevelopment.

The process that was subsequently followed for securing the various approvals for the arena's construction was plagued by difficulties and procedural irregularities. A group of citizens opposed the destruction of the Eaton's building and launched a grassroots campaign to save the building. In the face of governmental indifference to their arguments, they eventually sought judicial review of the decisions to permit demolition of the building and to issue the permits necessary for construction of the arena.

The efforts of the Save the Eaton's Building Coalition to use the courts to overturn the local planning decisions were largely unsuccessful. The Coalition's core argument was that the political process followed by the city was fundamentally flawed and that local decision-makers were biased and had not given the Coalition a fair hearing. In particular, they were concerned with the "head start" offered to the developer, which meant that alternative proposals for redeveloping the Eaton's site were not given a fair hearing. They also argued that the Historical Buildings Committee, which was required to issue an advisory opinion as to whether the Eaton's building should be listed as a protected property, was asked by city staff to delay considering the matter until after the City Property Committee had decided whether or not to recommend approval of the arena project. In the end the Historical Buildings Committee did recommend listing the Eaton's building, but by that point the Property Committee had voted in favour of the redevelopment project. Arguably, this might have been more difficult had the Historical Buildings Committee's report been issued prior to its deliberations. Finally, several city councillors, including members of the Property Committee, publicly announced their support for the project and dismissed the Coalition's arguments prior to formal hearings on the issue. Moreover, the city had actually signed a contract with the developer to take all necessary steps to secure the various permits and permissions necessary for the project to proceed.[22]

From the perspective of the Coalition, all these things added up to a process that was both flawed and stacked against them. It certainly appears that the city council had made up its mind to support the redevelopment, and the various hearings and committee deliberations were simply formalities. The courts, however, did not agree with the Coalition. While their decisions in the cases are quite complex, they can summarized as finding that municipal governments cannot be held to the same procedural standards as other administrative bodies. The very political nature of municipal governments means that members of adjudicative committees, such as the Property Committee, necessarily have opinions and viewpoints about the issues that come before them. Moreover, unlike most administrative bodies, those decisions may very well be publicly known and in some instances, may even have formed the basis of an election campaign. To treat these "pre-judgements" as a form of bias or bad faith on the part of the city, the court held, would prevent the city from functioning. In short, in this instance, the political nature of municipal governance meant that what would normally be considered unacceptable became unavoidable. As in the *Shell* case, the interests of local capital and local developers were left relatively undisturbed by the courts.

The Save the Eaton's Building Coalition cases demonstrate a number of the limitations of judicial review as a vehicle for political action. While the cases raised important points about the nature of local democracy, the administrative law principles in this area are extremely narrow and technical in nature. As a result, the judicial decisions tended to focus on a detailed analysis of the statutory mandate of the various city committees and the procedural requirements set out in the *City of Winnipeg Act*. The court applied a very formalistic approach to its interpretation of democracy. The legislature, it held, had given the city government the contradictory roles of a regulatory agency and a legislature at the same time. The court, therefore, accepted this and refused to examine more closely the integrity of the decision-making process.

More importantly, however, the decisions did little to enhance the capacity of the Save the Eaton's Building Coalition to frame its issues for the public and to appeal to a broader constituency. The technical nature of the property committee's procedural obligations did not lend themselves to exploring the broader issue of urban planning and alternatives to the city's vision of a redeveloped downtown. The Coalition had a number of ideas on this point; however, the court cases did not provide a forum for articulating those ideas to the public. In part, this is because of the area of law the Coalition was forced to engage with. Administrative law, as discussed above, is generally not concerned with substantive outcomes. As a result, the actual decision reached by the city—to permit construction of the arena—was never before the courts. In fact, the only issue under consideration was the much narrower one of the process by which the city had come to that decision. The Coalition, therefore, had a difficult time using the decision to launch a discussion of these broader issues of urban planning and to develop an alternative vision of the downtown.

The *Save the Eaton's Building Coalition* case also serves as a cautionary tale. In this instance, the Coalition devoted almost all of its time and resources to the court cases. This was in part because the political battle at the level of the city government had already been lost. Going to court was the only mechanism available to prevent the actual demolition of the building. At the same time, however, the Coalition might have been more successful had it developed a broader and more diverse strategy. While it tried in the early stages of the campaign to do this, the logic of the court cases appears to have overwhelmed it. This may also be a result of the structure of the Coalition itself. The Save the Eaton's Building Coalition was formed for the sole purpose of saving the building. It was a single-issue group, without a broader political agenda. Its membership came from a diverse range of groups and individuals, many of whom were united only by the desire to prevent the building being destroyed. For groups of this kind, the court battle can serve as a unifying force where no others exist, but it can also make the development of a broader political agenda difficult.

Conclusion

The administrative state provides numerous opportunities for social action groups to challenge state policy and to involve themselves in a wide range of regulatory and policy debates. Participation at this level offers some advantages. It is often less expensive than going to court, and the policy outcomes of particular cases may be more tangible. At the same time, however, administrative decisions may be more limited than judicial decisions and will generally have less scope for broad media attention. As well, there may be less opportunity for challenging unfavourable administrative decisions. At the same time, social action groups may have little choice but to appear before these boards and tribunals. Whole spheres of policy have effectively been delegated to administrative agencies. Trade unions, for example, cannot ignore labour reviews, and environmental groups must participate in environmental assessment reviews. In these instances, participating before these quasi-judicial boards and tribunals is not so much a deliberate attempt to pursue judicialized or legalized politics, but rather part of an attempt to affect state decision-making and influence policy development. For the social action group, however, it is important to be aware of the role of these boards and tribunals, and the opportunities and limits of appearing before them.

Notes

1. For an excellent discussion of the historical origins of Keynesianism and its policy implications, see John Shields and B. Mitchell Evans, *Shrinking the State: Globalization and Public Administration "Reform"* (Halifax: Fernwood

Publishing, 1998), ch. 1.

2. Claus Offe, *Contradictions of the Welfare State*, (Cambridge: MIT Press, 1984).

3. The mandate of the CRTC is to regulate all aspects of the broadcasting and telecommunications industries in Canada. See <www.crtc.gc.ca>.

4. See *Wedekind. v. Director of Income Maintenance Branch (Ont.)* (1994),75 O.A.C. 358.

5. For more details see the National Energy Board's Web site, <www.neb-one.gc.ca>.

6. A similar structure is frequently used for arbitration hearings that deal with grievances over the administration of a collective agreement.

7. The *United Nations Convention on Refugees* defines a refugee as a person who, by reason of a well-founded fear of persecution based on race, religion, nationality, membership in a particular social action group, or political opinion, has fled her home country and is unable to return because of that fear.

8. See Joan Sherman and Michael Gismondi, "Not Directly Affected: Using the Law to Close the Door on Environmentalists," *Journal of Canadian Studies* 31 (1996), p. 102–19.

9. Private bar lawyers are generally uninterested in providing services in the area of poverty law. As a result, advocacy in this area is usually provided by community legal clinics or community-based organizations and self-help centres. See B. Sheldrick, "Law, Representation, and Political Activism: Community-based Practice and the Mobilization of Legal Resources," *Canadian Journal of Law and Society* 10 (1995), 155–84.

10. Details of CELA's activities can be found at <www.cela.ca>.

11. A.V. Dicey, *Introduction to the Study of the Law of the Constitution* (London: MacMillan, 1902). For an excellent discussion of Dicey's legacy, see Harry Arthurs, "Rethinking Administrative Law: A Slightly Dicey Business," *Osgoode Hall Law Journal* 17 (1979), p. 1–45, and the collection of essays edited by Bob Fine, *Democracy and the Rule of Law* (London: Pluto Press, 1984).

12. See, for example, *Metropolitan Life Insurance Co. v. International Union of Operating Engineers, Local 796* [1970] SCR 425; and *Canadian Union of Public Employees, Local 963 v. New Brunswick Liquor Corp.*, [1979] 2 S.C.R. 227 (SCC).

13. *Anisminic Ltd. v. Foreign Compensation Commission* [1969] 2 AC 147 (House of Lords).

14. *Canadian Union of Public Employees v. New Brunswick Liquor Corp.*, supra. note 12.

15. *Pezim v. British Columbia (Superintendant of Brokers)* [1994] 2 S.C.R. 557.

16. The Canadian Federation of Municipalities, at its 2001 annual conference, adopted a resolution calling for municipalities to be made an autonomous order of government with full constitutional status. See Canadian Federation of Municipalities, *Joint FCM/CAMA Task Force on the Future Role of*

Municipal Government, May 2001, available at <www.fcm.ca/newfcm/Java/ frame.htm>.

17. For an interesting look at the experience of the Greater London Council, see Maureen MacKintosh and Hilary Wainwright (eds.), *A Taste of Power: The Politics of Local Government* (London: Verso, 1987).

18. *Shell Canada Products v. City of Vancouver* (1994) 1 DLR (4th) 1.

19. Ibid, p. 18.

20. Ibid, p. 31.

21. Eaton's was a national chain with department stores in most major Canadian cities. The Winnipeg store was one of the oldest and an excellent example of turn-of-the-century architecture.

22. The factual background can be found in the court judgements by Justice MacInnes. See *Save the Eaton's Building Coalition v. the City of Winnipeg and True North Partnership* (August 10, 2001) available at <www.canlii.org/mb/ cas/mbqb/2001/2001mbqb206.html> and *Save the Eaton's Building Coalition v. the City of Winnipeg* (June 4, 2002), available at <www.canlii.org/mb/ cas/mbqb/2002/2002mbqb165.html>.

Chapter 7

Conclusion

The relationship between law and political activism continues to be hotly debated. This book has tried to shift the terms of that debate. The overwhelming focus of academic inquiry has been on the courts and the broad question of whether they can be or should be agents of social change. While academics worry about these matters, groups seeking social equality and social justice continue to use the law and the courts, sometimes with great success and sometimes not. The real question is not whether courts are advantageous to social action groups, or whether more cases have been won or lost, or whether there are more democratic forms of political activism, or whether lawyers and judges will co-opt the struggles of activists. For social action groups, the real question is how does law intersect with the struggle for justice and equality.

The practice of social action groups seems to have little to do with the debates that take place in academic circles. Social movements are not concerned that courts are less democratic than legislatures. To these activists the halls of legislature are venues for the rich and privileged to exert control. The rich and privileged may also have advantages in courtrooms, as Galanter rightly pointed out almost thirty years ago. The "haves" do in fact enjoy significant advantages in the judicial arena. For groups arguing that the organization of our society is fundamentally unjust, this would come as no surprise. The activists who took on McDonald's in the McLibel case knew that the odds were stacked against them. When George Harris and CHO!CES decided to use the courts to challenge Revenue Canada, they knew the case was doubtful. For most social activists, however, the fact that the courts are undemocratic does not distinguish them from many other institutions of the state.

The undemocratic nature of law has largely been the focus of left-wing legal academics, particularly those who see law as an instrument of social control and the tool of elites. There is much that must be taken seriously in this argument. However, focusing on the undemocratic character of courts leads us away from our primary concern: namely, the pursuit of social justice. Instead of examining how law and courts might contribute to that pursuit, the argument becomes focused on the fact that lawyers and judges are members of an elite, and that judges are unelected. The quest begins for a purer, more democratic, more authentic politics. Instead, we should be maximizing opportunities to advance claims for social justice in a political and economic structure that is frequently hostile and unreceptive to these claims.

Democracy and democratic practice must be at the heart of any campaign for social justice. However, we should seek the locus of democratic practice in the actions and processes of the social movements, not within the state. While campaigns to democratize the state and make policy processes more participatory and inclusive may be important within social justice struggles, it is wrong to judge the legitimacy of social and political activism by the democratic character of the state institutions against which and within which groups must struggle.

This broadens our focus beyond courts to the practice of social action groups struggling for equality and justice. It also leads us away from our preoccupation with the question of whether or not the courts can produce social change. The focus on social change is misplaced. While "social change" may often be used synonymously with "social justice," it is, in fact, a value-neutral term that ignores the wide range of ideological positions seeking some degree of social change. Many of those groups are fighting for social change that would move the struggle for justice backward: those seeking to criminalize poverty and homelessness, to reduce or eliminate public heath care and public education, or to reverse equality gains made by women, Aboriginal people, or gays and lesbians. It also wrongly casts the courts as the agent of change rather than the groups that seek to mobilize around issues of social justice.

The point here is that courts and the law form part of the tactical resources available to social action groups. We need to situate legal tactics within the broader struggle for social justice. Going to court will never secure social change, nor will it achieve social justice. It may, however, be an important tool within a broader struggle for social justice. Victories in court may be important. Certainly Aboriginal people in Canada, and gay and lesbian activists can point to specific court decisions that have advanced their struggles for equality. Indeed, it would be completely wrong to fault these efforts because they had not resulted in clear victories or social change. Gains made in court will always be partial. They need to be advanced through struggle and political action directed both at the state and at society. Gains also have to be defended against those who would seek to roll them back.

In this sense, court decisions are simply milestones in the struggles for social justice taking place not just in the court but in a wide variety of sites. There is no preferred social or political site for these struggles. They occur in legislatures and bureaucracies, workplaces, housing shelters, church basements, families, universities, in books, in conversations in coffee shops, in the streets and in the courts. The Ontario Coalition Against Poverty entitled its guide to the law, *In the Streets and in the Courts: We Fight to Win*—underlying the range of settings in which claims for social justice can be made. Engagement with the law and the courts must not be seen as the purpose of political activism, but rather as part of a broader campaign for social change. It must be combined with lobbying government, demonstrations and protests, and community based mobilization and politicization. Going to court can never substitute for these things, and it is precisely for this reason that the most successful excursions into the legal realm are part of a broader political strategy.

The potential of law to depoliticize and demobilize is real and should not be taken lightly. It is the grounding of a legal strategy within a broader political campaign that enables groups to resist these tendencies. The exclusivity of legal knowledge and expertise makes the legal terrain a far more difficult one for social action groups to navigate. Claims for social justice must often be translated into legal terminology and reframed in a language that is acceptable to the courts. While the law often does create and reproduce inequality, its ideology also rests on notions of justice, equality and fairness, which are malleable and can be exploited by social action groups to advance claims for social justice. The law is not, in this regard, a total sham. If claims for social justice are not entertained, or if they are dismissed too routinely, the legitimacy of courts will be undermined. If the courts are to be perceived as just, they must sometimes actually be just.

For social action groups, the difficulty is in navigating the legal terrain without becoming lost in it. The objective of this book is to assist groups in developing tactical, rather than substantive, expertise. It certainly is not my intention to turn activists into lawyers. However, activists do need enough expertise and knowledge to make sound tactical decisions about how and when to engage with law. This also enhances their capacity to retain control in a legal challenge and resist the temptation to allow the lawyer to handle it.

Some degree of legal expertise may be helpful for activists and social action groups even where there are no plans to pursue a litigation strategy. As discussed in Chapter 3, the state frequently uses the law to regulate and restrict the expression of dissent. Activists frequently find themselves on the wrong side of the law, possibly facing criminal charges. In this context it is important to understand that law, in its coercive and repressive form, may affect struggles for social justice. A criminal trial may involve more than a simple consideration of whether the elements of the offence have been proven, and may become a forum and focus for broader issues of social justice.

It is, of course, impossible to provide a blueprint for social justice. What is possible, however, is to identify the sorts of cases that would benefit from a strategy of engagement with the law. Law may usefully be invoked in a number of different situations and contexts. Cases of unequal or differential treatment always raise the possibility of a rights-based legal dimension. Cases of overt discrimination, or the application of state power in a differential or abusive fashion, or the development of policies that exclude certain segments of the population all raise equality claims. These arguments can be forcefully made, particularly where those who have been excluded come from historically disenfranchised or disempowered groups. The poor, visible minorities, women and Aboriginal persons, for example, are all in a position to exploit the language of equity, fairness and rights to advance their claims for social justice. This does not mean simply going to court. Rather, it involves creating a political strategy and a practice that utilize concepts of justice and rights to highlight the grievances the group has suffered and to advance substantive alternatives to the current political and social order.

Depending on the specific nature of those claims, engaging with the courts may be a useful strategy. In other instances it may be counter-productive. The key, however, is for groups not to insist that some political strategies are acceptable while others are not, but rather to understand when to pursue one strategy and not another, and how a multiplicity of strategies and tactics can be woven into a coherent campaign for social justice. In this regard, much may depend on the nature of the social action group involved—its capacities and resources—but also on the political situation that confronts the group.

Before embarking on a strategy of legal activism, a number of tactical questions should be considered:

- Does the case raise broad issues of rights and justice, or does it involve more narrow or technical legal issues? It may be more difficult for social action groups to maintain control over the latter sort of case, which will usually involve a greater reliance on the technical expertise of lawyers.

- To what extent can the legal issues raised by the case be incorporated into the group's political framework? Another way of posing this question is to ask whether the group's political agenda can be framed in legal language that is acceptable to the courts but doesn't compromise the group's principles. It may be that going to court requires too great a sacrifice. This question will frequently be easier to answer in groups with a fairly coherent political ideology. In coalitions, on the other hand, where a consistent ideological position may be lacking, it may be difficult to reach a consensus on these questions.

- What is the likelihood of success in the courts? Going to court is an expensive proposition and a reasonable chance of success will make it easier to justify the expenditure of time and resources. There may, however, be instances where it makes sense politically to pursue a case even though the chances of success are slim.

- How important is the issue for the overall political objectives of the group? Is it at the core of the group's political ambitions? Challenging anti-abortion legislation, for example, is clearly critical to the overall political objectives of pro-choice groups. On the other hand, for an anti-poverty group launching a challenge to the most recent round of welfare cuts, it may be important, but it will not be central to the group's overall project. It may be more important for the group to pursue state support for community development initiatives.

- Who is the intended target of the litigation? The target may not be the same as the defendant in the court action. The case may be intended to reach a broad public audience or it may be aimed at a narrower constituency. If the purpose of the litigation is to raise public awareness of an injustice, or to sway public opinion, a careful assessment is needed as to whether the litigation can actually advance this goal. Groups must also consider how to combine the litigation with strategies that attract the media and public attention.

- How much time and how many resources will the case take? The group must ask itself whether it can afford to pursue this strategy. Going to court will be costly, both financially and in terms of the time and energy expended by group members. There are, however, ways to reduce the costs of litigation. The group may have legal expertise or knowledge within its ranks, perhaps as the result of a previous engagement in legal activism, or through group members with legal background and expertise. These resources can supplement and reduce some of the costs of litigation. The group may have other useful resources and expertise as well. Writing pamphlets, preparing public education materials and designing Web sites are all important vehicles by which the group's underlying political agenda can be communicated.

- Can the group form an alliance or coalition with other groups interested in supporting the litigation or possessing needed legal expertise?
- Are there legal clinics or other community-based legal resources available to assist in pursuing the litigation? Community-based legal clinics and activist lawyers committed to social justice can be important resources. Social action groups may be able to form alliances and coalitions with these sources of legal expertise, effectively integrating law into the group's ongoing repertoire of political action. Coalitions of this sort can be difficult to maintain. In many respects, though, they are similar to the networks and alliances that exist between a host of social welfare "professionals"—community economic development practitioners, social workers, literacy workers—and grassroots political organizations. There may be tangible benefits to seeking out this sort of legal organization as opposed to simply hiring a high-profile lawyer from a large firm. Utilizing this sort of legal expertise may decrease the risks of co-optation by the conservative tendencies of law and legal ideology.
- Will the case take too many resources away from the group's other political activities? Pursuing a court case to the final stages of appeal can be an all-consuming affair. Members of the group may have to devote too much of their time to supporting the case, with detrimental consequences for the group's other activities.
- Is it possible to integrate fundraising and litigation support into a campaign of mobilization that can be used to keep the membership engaged or even to expand the membership of the group?

The decision to go to court is a big one and should not be taken lightly. Legal strategy is fraught with difficulty and requires large expenditures of time and resources. Moreover, even if successful, there will still be a need for ongoing political engagement. Having said this, activist groups frequently see themselves as having little choice but to go to court. In some instances this is because other forms of dissent have led to criminal charges. There may be times when the only way to assert a right is to actually violate the law and invite the state to prosecute. Aboriginal groups, for example, have found that in order to assert their rights as a people, they must break laws and regulations that prohibit them from engaging in traditional activities.

The failure of democratic institutions makes recourse to the law one of the few tactics left to some groups. Lobbying, protests, petitions and letter-writing campaigns often prove ineffective. Groups seeking social justice frequently lack the resources of elites in society and consequently have limited access to the so-called "democratic" political institutions of our society. Going to court is often a last resort. Of course, it would be better if we had genuinely democratic institutions through which claims of social justice could be heard. This would be preferable to legal activism. Groups committed to social justice should continue to push for genuine democratic reform. Until that day arrives, however, and perhaps even afterwards, social activists will continue to confront the law. Its contradictory nature pushes activists into the judicial arena even as they resist its coercive and conservative tendencies. Its language of justice, equality and fairness provides a powerful tool. The law is more than mere rhetoric and has a substantive reality that makes it a potential resource for advancing social justice claims. Social action groups need to navigate this contradiction, exploiting the possibilities while remaining wary of the pitfalls.

Appendix 1

On-Line Legal Research Tools

Constitutional Documents

Canadian Charter of Rights and Freedoms: <www.laws.justice.gc.ca/en/charter/index.html>
American Bill of Rights: <www.law.cornell.edu/constitution/constitution.billofrights.html>
European Convention on Human Rights: <www.echr.coe.int>
United Kingdom Human Rights Act: <www.hmso.gov.uk/acts/acts1998/19980042.htm>

Canada

Canadian Legal Information Institute:
An excellent database that is fully searchable and provides access to statutes, regulations and case law for Canada, the provinces and territories.
The Federal Department of Justice:
Access to Justice Network:
A searchable database of resources on a wide range of legal topics.
Supreme Court of Canada: <www.lexum.umontreal.ca/csc-scc/en/>
A searchable database of Supreme Court decisions since 1986.
University of Toronto Bora Laskin Law Library: <www.law-lib.utoronto.ca/resources/>
Most law libraries have a list of legal resources and Internet-based research tools. The Bora Laskin Law Library's is one of the best and most comprehensive, both for Canadian and international legal materials.
Jurist Canada:
A database of resources and links relating to a wide range of legal topics.

United States

Legal Information Institute:
Housed at Cornell University, it's all you really need. An excellent source for federal and state law, decisions by the United States Supreme Court, federal courts and state courts. Fully searchable.
Findlaw: <www.findlaw.com>
A useful search engine.

Europe

Acts of the UK Parliament: <www.hmso.gov.uk/acts.htm>
United Kingdom Bill of Rights cases: <www.beagle.org.uk. >
This site provides a good summary of human rights cases and a searchable database of *European Convention on Human Rights* articles and U.K. case law.
Britain and Ireland Legal Information Institute: <www.bailii.org/databases.html#ew>
Access to United Kingdom Judicial decisions for the House of Lords, Court of Appeal and High Court. However, online decisions only go back to 1996.
European Court of Human Rights decisions: <www.echr.coe.int>
European Union Law: <europa.eu.int/cj/en/index.html>

Feminist Legal Resources

Legal Resources for Women: <www.ibiblio.org/cheryb/women/resource/legal-int.html>
Canadian Women's Studies On-line Law: <www.utoronto.ca/womens/legal.htm>
A database of a wide range of sources dealing with women and the law.

Lesbian and Gay Legal Resources

And Justice for All: <qrd.tcp.com/qrd/www/orgs/aja/legal.htm>
ALGA Europe:
Queer Legal Resources: <www.qrd.org/qrd/www/legal/>
National Journal of Sexual Orientation Law: <www.ibiblio.org/gaylaw/>

International Legal Resources:

JusticeLink: <www.kcl.ac.uk/depsta/rel/ccjs/justicelink/>
The Centre for Crime and Justice Studies provides an extensive guide to criminal justice resources on the Web.
Amnesty International: <www.amnesty.org>
NGO Global Network: <www.ngo.org/index2.htm>
A Web site of NGOs associated with the United Nations
Global Legal Information Network (GLIN): <www.loc.gov/law/glin/>
Maintained by the Library of Congress, GLIN is an extensive database of laws, regulations and other legal documents from around the world.
University Law Review Project:
A searchable database of on-line law journals.
Human Rights Watch:
An International NGO devoted to monitoring human rights through-out the world.
Human Rights Internet: <www.hri.ca/welcome.asp>
University of Minnesota Human Rights Library: <www1.umn.edu/humanrts/>
Derechos Human Rights:

Legal Aid and Public Legal Education Sources

Legal Aid Around the World: <www.ptla.org/ptlasite/links/international.htm>
From Pine Tree Legal Assistance, a law centre assisting low-income people in the state of Maine, this Web site provides an extensive list of legal aid clinics, law centres and public legal education organizations throughout the world. Coverage includes the United States, Europe, Canada, Africa, Asia, Australia, New Zealand, South America and Israel.

References

Antonyshyn, Patricia, B. Lee and Alex Merrill. 1988. "Marching for Women's Lives: The Campaign for Free Standing Abortion Clinics in Ontario." In Frank Cunningham et. al. (eds.), *Social Movements/Social Change: The Politics and Practice of Organizing*. Toronto: Between the Lines.

Arthurs, Harry. 1979. "Rethinking Administrative Law: A Slightly Dicey Business." *Osgoode Hall Law Journal* 17, 1.

Aylward, Carol. 1999. *Canadian Critical Race Theory: Racism and the Law*. Halifax: Fernwood Publishing.

Bartholomew, Amy, and Alan Hunt. 1990. "What's Wrong With Rights?" *Law and Inequality* 9.

Bell, Stewart. 2003. "CSIS Paints Anti-Trade Movement as Menace: Top-Secret Report Warns of Violent and Extreme Elements." *National Post* Feb. 24, A1.

Bellow, Gary, and Jeanne Kettleson. 1978. "From Ethics to Politics: Confronting Scarcity and Fairness in Public Interest Practice." *Boston University Law Review* 58.

Black, Errol, and Jim Silver. 2001. *Building a Better World: An Introduction to Unionism in Canada*. Halifax: Fernwood Publishing.

Borrows, John. 1997. "Contemporary Traditional Equality: The Effect of the Charter on First Nations Politics." In David Schneiderman and Kate Sutherland (eds.), *Charting the Consequences: The Impact of Charter Rights on Canadian Law and Politics*. Toronto: University of Toronto Press.

Bourdieu, Pierre. 1987. "The Force of Law: Toward a Sociology of the Juridical Field." *The Hastings Law Journal* 38, 5.

Boyle, Chris. 1988. "The 'Irrationality' of the State: The Nielson Report as a Challenge to Left Analysis." *Studies in Political Economy* 27.

Brickey S., and E. Comack. 1987. "The Rule of Law in Social Transformation: Is a Jurisprudence of Insurgency Possible?" *Canadian Journal of Law and Society* 2.

Brodie, Janine, Shelley Gavigan and Jane Jenson. 1992. *The Politics of Abortion*. Toronto: Oxford University Press.

Busby, Karen. 2000. "Raising the Dough: Funding For Lawyers at Public Inquiries." In W. Pue (ed.), *Pepper in Our Eyes: The APEC Affair*. Vancouver: UBC Press.

Cairns, Alan. 1992. *Charter versus Federalism: The Dilemmas of Constitutional Reform*. Montreal, Kingston: McGill-Queen's University Press.

California Anti-SLAPP Project. *Survival Guide for SLAPP Victims*. Available at

<www.casp.net/survival.html>. Accessed on February 2, 2004.

Campbell, Duncan. 2003. "Forty Injured as Police Fire Rubber Bullets at Peace Protesters." *The Guardian*. April 8. Available at <www.guardian.co.uk/antiwar/story/0,12809,932145,00.html>. Accessed on November 12, 2003.

Cassels, Jamie, and Maureen Maloney. 1990. "Critical Legal Education: Paralysis with a Purpose." *Canadian Journal of Law and Society* 4.

Chouinard, Vera. 1998. "Challenging Law's Empire: Rebellion, Incorporation, and Changing Geographics of Power in Ontario's Legal Clinic System." *Studies in Political Economy* 55.

Cohen, Maxwell. 1968. "Human Rights: Programme or Catchall? A Canadian Rationale." *Canadian Bar Review* 46.

della Porta, Donatella, and Herbert Reiter. 1988. "The Policing of Protest in Western Democracies." In Donatella della Porta and Herbert Reiter (eds.), *Policing Protest: The Control of Mass Demonstrations in Western Democracies.* Minneapolis: University of Minnesota Press.

Dicey, A.V. 1902. *Introduction to the Study of the Law of the Constitution.* London: MacMillan.

Dworkin, Ronald. 1977. *Taking Rights Seriously.* Cambridge: Harvard University Press.

Epp, Charles. 1999. "The Two Motifs in Galanter's 'Why the Haves Come Out Ahead.'" *Law and Society Review* 33, 4.

_____. 1998. *The Rights Revolution: Lawyers, Activists, and Supreme Courts in Comparative Perspective.* Chicago: University of Chicago Press.

Ewick, Patricia, and Susan Silbey. 1999. "Common Knowledge and Ideological Critique: The Significance of Knowing that the 'Haves' Come Out Ahead." *Law and Society Review* 33, 4.

Fillieule, Olivier, and Fabien Jobard. 1998. "The Policing of Protest in France: Toward a Model of Protest Policing." In Donatella della Porta and Herbert Reiter (eds.), *Policing Protest: The Control of Mass Demonstrations in Western Democracies.* Minneapolis: University of Minnesota Press.

Fine, Bob. 1984. *Democracy and the Rule of Law.* London: Pluto Press.

Fitzgerald, Patrick, and Barry Wright. 2000. *Looking at Law: Canada's Legal System.* Toronto: Butterworths.

Freeman, Alan. 1990. "Anti-discrimination Law: The View from 1989." In David Kairys (ed.), *The Politics of Law: A Progressive Critique.* New York: Pantheon Books.

Friedlander, Lara. 1995. "Costs and the Public Interest Litigant." *McGill Law Journal* 40.

Fudge, Judy, and Harry Glasbeek. 1992. "The Politics of Rights: A Politics with Little Class." *Social and Legal Studies* 1.

Galanter, Marc. 1974. "Why the Haves Come out Ahead: Speculations on the Limits of Legal Change." *Law and Society Review* 9.

Gavigan, Shelley. 1992. "Morgentaler and Beyond: Abortion, Reproduction and the Courts." In Janine Brodie, Shelley Gavigan and Jane Jenson (eds.),

The Politics of Abortion. Toronto: Oxford University Press.

Gewirtz, P. 1983. "Remedies and Resistance." *Yale Law Journal* 92.

Gibson, Dale. 1982. "The Charter of Rights and the Private Sector." *Manitoba Law Journal* 12.

Granfield, Robert. 1992. *Making Elite Lawyers: Visions of Law at Harvard and Beyond.* New York: Routledge.

Griffith, John. 1993. "The Rights Stuff." In Ralph Miliband and Leo Panitch (eds.), *Real Problems, False Solutions, Socialist Register.* London: Merlin Press.

Grossman, Joel, Herbert Kritzer and Stewart Macaulay. 1999. "Do the 'Haves' Still Come Out Ahead?" *Law and Society Review* 33, 4.

Guardian Unlimited. 2003. "Pupils Prominent in Global Anti-War Marches." March 24. Available at <www.guardian.co.uk/antiwar/story/0,12809,920898,00.html>. Accessed on November 12, 2003.

_____. 2003. "Thousands Join Anti-War Demos." March 23. Available at <www.guardian.co.uk/antiwar/story/0,12809,919813,00.html>. Accessed on November 12, 2003.

Handler, Joel. 1978. *Social Movements and the Legal System: A Theory of Law Reform and Social Change.* New York: Academic Press.

Hein, Gregory. 2000. *Interest Group Litigation and Canadian Democracy.* Montreal: Institute for Research on Public Policy.

Heron, Craig. 1996. *The Canadian Labour Movement: A Short History.* Toronto: J. Lorimer.

Herman, Didi. 1997. "The Good, The Bad, and the Smugly: Sexual Orientation and Perspectives on the Charter." In David Schneiderman and Kate Sutherland (eds.), *Charting the Consequences: The Impact of Charter Rights on Canadian Law and Politics.* Toronto: University of Toronto Press.

_____. 1993. "Beyond the Rights Debate." *Social and Legal Studies* 2.

Hiebert, Janet. 1999. *Wrestling with Rights: Judges, Parliament and the Making of Social Policy.* Montreal: Institute for Research on Public Policy.

_____. 1996. *Limiting Rights: The Dilemma of Judicial Review.* Montreal: McGill-Queen's University Press.

Hudson, Edward. 2003. "We Have a Duty to Disobey." *Winnipeg Free Press,* March 2.

Hunt, Alan. 1990. "Rights and Social Movements: Counter-Hegemonic Strategies." *Journal of Law and Society* 17.

Hunt, Murray. 1997. *Using Human Rights Law in English Courts.* Oxford: Hart Publishing.

Hutchinson, Allan, and Andrew Petter. 1988. "Private Rights/Public Wrongs: The Liberal Lie of the Charter." *University of Toronto Law Journal* 38.

International Civil Liberties Monitoring Group. 2003. "In the Shadow of Law: Report by the International Civil Liberties Monitoring Group in Response to Justice Canada's 1st Annual Report on the Application of the Anti-Terrorism Act (Bill C-36)." *CAUT Bulletin* 50, 6.

Johnson, Lois. 1991. "The New Public Interest Law: From Old Theories to a

New Agenda." *Boston University Public Interest Law Journal* 1.

Kelly, James. 1999. "Bureaucratic Activism and the Charter of Rights and Freedoms: The Department of Justice and its Entry into the Centre of Government." *Canadian Public Administration* 42, 4.

Kinsman, Gary, Dieter K. Buse and Mercedes Steedman (eds.). 2000. *Whose National Security? Canadian State Surveillance and the Creation of Enemies.* Toronto: Between the Lines Press.

Kweit, Mary, and Robert Kweit. 1980. "Bureaucratic Decision-Making: Impediments to Citizen Participation." *Polity* 12.

Larson, Magali Sarfatti. 1989. "The Changing Functions of Lawyers in the Liberal State: Reflections for Comparative Analysis." In Richard Abel and Philip Lewis (eds.), *Lawyers in Society: Comparative Theories.* Berkeley: University of California Press.

_____. 1977. *The Rise of Professionalism: A Sociological Analysis.* Berkeley: University of California Press.

Lempert, Richard. 1999. "A Classic at 25: Reflections on Galanter's 'Haves' Article and Work It Inspired." *Law and Society Review* 33, 4.

Leys, Colin. 2001. *Market Driven Politics: Neoliberal Democracy and the Public Interest.* London: Verso.

MacKintosh, Maureen, and Hilary Wainwright (eds.). 1987. *A Taste of Power: The Politics of Local Government.* London: Verso

Macpherson, C.B. 1977. *The Life and Times of Liberal Democracy.* Oxford: Oxford University Press.

Makin, Kirk. 2002. "We are not Gunslingers." *Globe and Mail.* April 9.

Mandel, Michael. 1994. *The Charter of Rights and the Legalization of Politics in Canada.* Toronto: Wall and Thompson.

Mansell, Wade, Belinda Meteyard and Alan Thomson. 1995. *A Critical Introduction to Law.* London: Cavendish Publishing Ltd.

Mather, Lynn, and Barbara Yngvesson. 1980. "Language, Audience and the Transformation of Disputes." *Law and Society Review* 15.

Maynes, Clifford. 1989. *Public Consultation: A Citizens Handbook.* Toronto: Ontario Environment Network.

McCann, Michael W. 1991. "Legal Mobilization and Social Reform Movements: Notes on Theory and Its Applications." *Studies in Law, Politics and Society* 11.

McCann, Michael W., and Helena Silverstein. 1993. "Social Movements and the American State: Legal Mobilization as a Strategy for Democratization." In Gregory Albo, David Langille and Leo Panitch (eds.), *A Different Kind of State? Popular Power and Democratic Administration.* Toronto: Oxford University Press.

McIntyre, Mike. 2003. "Mountie-Killing Case Begins: Police Furious over Being Frozen out of Challenge." *Winnipeg Free Press*, February 26.

McKay, Wayne. 2001. "The Legislature, the Executive and the Courts: The Delicate Balance of Power or Who Is Running This Country Anyway?"

Dalhousie Law Journal 24.

McLeod, Ian. 1996. *Legal Method*. London: MacMillan Press.

McNeil, Kent. 2001. *Emerging Justice: Essays on Indigenous Rights in Canada and Australia*. Saskatoon: University of Saskatchewan Native Law Centre.

———. 1996. "Aboriginal Governments and the Canadian Charter of Rights and Freedoms." *Osgoode Hall Law Journal* 34, 1.

McPhail, Clark, David Schweingruber and John McCarthy. 1998. "Policing Protest in the United States: 1960–1995." In Donatella della Porta and Herbert Reiter (eds.), *Policing Protest: The Control of Mass Demonstrations in Western Democracies*. Minneapolis: University of Minnesota Press.

Merry, Sally. 1988. "Legal Pluralism." *Law and Society Review* 22, 5.

Mia, Ziyaad. 2002. "Terrorizing the Rule of Law: Implications of the Anti-Terrorism Act." *National Journal of Constitutional Law* 14, 1.

Milner, Neil. 1988. "The Dilemmas of Legal Mobilization: Ideologies and Strategies of Mental Patient Liberation Groups." *Law and Policy* 8.

Morton, F.L., and Rainer Knopff. 2000. *The Charter Revolution and the Court Party*. Peterborough: Broadview Press.

Mosher, Janet. 1997. "Legal Education: Nemesis or Ally of Social Movements?" *Osgoode Hall Law Journal* 35.

Muldoon, P. 1989. *The Law of Intervention: Status and Practice*. Aurora, Ontario: Canada Law Book.

National Council of Welfare. 1995. *Legal Aid and the Poor*. Ottawa: National Council of Welfare.

Nelson, Robert L., and David M. Trubek. 1992. "Arenas of Professionalism: The Professional Ideologies of Lawyers in Context." In Robert Nelson, David Trubek and Rayman Solomon (eds.), *Lawyers' Ideals/Lawyers' Practices: Transformations in the American Legal Profession*. Ithaca: Cornell University Press.

Offe, Claus. 1984. *Contradictions of the Welfare State*. Cambridge: MIT Press.

Ontario Coalition Against Poverty. 2001. *In the Streets and in the Courts—We Fight to Win: A Legal Guide for Activists*. Available at <www.ocap.ca/archive/legalguide/>. Accessed on 09/11/03.

Panitch, Leo, and Donald Swartz. 2003. *From Consent to Coercion: The Assault on Trade Union Freedoms*. 3rd edition. Toronto: Garamond Press.

Pearlston, Karen. 2000. "APEC Days at UBC: Student Protests and National Security in an Era of Trade Liberalization." In Garry Kinsman, Dieter Buse and Mercedes Steedman (eds.), *Whose National Security? Canadian State Surveillance and the Creation of Enemies*. Toronto: Between the Lines Press.

Petter, Andrew. 1986. "The Politics of the Charter." *Supreme Court Law Review* 3.

Poulantzas, Nicos. 1978. *State, Power, Socialism*. London: New Left Books.

Pring, George, and Penelope Canan. 1996. *SLAPPs: Getting Sued for Speaking Out*. Philadelphia: Temple University Press.

Pue, Wes (ed). 2000. *Pepper in Our Eyes: The APEC Affair*. Vancouver: UBC Press.

Pugliese, David, and Jim Bronskill. 2001. "Keeping the Public in Check: Special Mountie Team, Police Tactics Threaten the Right to Free Speech and Assembly." *Ottawa Citizen*, August 18.

_____. 2001. "How Police Deter Dissent: Government Critics Decry Intimidation." *Ottawa Citizen*, August 21.

Quigley, Tim. 2003. "A Sweeping Assault on Civil Rights and Liberties: New Anti-Terrorist Bills Could Criminalize Political Dissent." *The CCPA Monitor*, April 9.

Razack, Sherene. 1991. *Canadian Feminism and the Law: The Women's Legal Education and Action Fund and the Pursuit of Equality*. Toronto: Second Story Press.

Reiner, Robert. 1998. "Policing, Protest and Disorder in Britain." In Donatella della Porta and Herbert Reiter (eds.), *Policing Protest: The Control of Mass Demonstrations in Western Democracies*. Minneapolis: University of Minnesota Press.

Roach, Kent. 2003. *September 11: Consequences for Canada*. Montreal: McGill-Queen's University Press.

_____. 1994. *Constitutional Remedies in Canada*. Aurora, Ont.: Canada Law Book.

Rogerson, Carol. "The Judicial Search for Appropriate Remedies under the Charter: The Examples of Overbreadth and Vagueness." In Robert Sharpe (ed.), *Charter Litigation*. Toronto: Butterworths.

Rosenberg, Gerald. 1991. *The Hollow Hope: Can Courts Bring about Social Change?* Chicago: University of Chicago Press.

Royal Canadian Mounted Police. Final report of the RCMP Public Complaints Commission. Ottawa: Government of Canada. Available at <www.cpc-cpp.gc.ca/>. Accessed on February 2, 2004.

Russell, Bob. 1997. "Reinventing a Labour Movement?" In William Carroll (ed.), *Organizing Dissent: Contemporary Social Movements in Theory and Practice*. Toronto: Garamond Press.

Santos, Boaventura de Sousa. 1992. "State, Law and Community in the World System: An Introduction." *Social and Legal Studies* 1.

_____. 1982. "Law and Community: the Changing Nature of State Power in Late Capitalism." In Richard Abel (ed.), *The Politics of Informal Justice*. New York: Academic Press.

Sarat, Austin, and Stuart Scheingold. 1998. "Cause Lawyering and the Reproduction of Professional Authority." In Austin Sarat and Stuart Scheingold (eds.), *Cause Lawyering: Political Commitments and Professional Responsibilities*. Oxford: Oxford University Press.

Saunders, Doug. 2003. "U.S. Top Court Backs Anti-Abortion Activists." *Globe and Mail*, Feb. 27.

Scheingold, Stuart. 1989. "Constitutional Rights and Social Change: Civil Rights in Perspective." In Michael McCann and Gerald Houseman (eds.), *Judging the Constitution: Critical Essays on Judicial Law Making*. Glenview:

Scott, Foresman and Co.

Schneider, Elizabeth. 1986. "The Dialectics of Rights and Politics: Perspectives from the Women's Movement." *New York University Law Review* 61.

Schneiderman, David, and Brenda Cossman. 2001. "Political Association and the Anti-Terrorism Bill." In Ronald J. Daniels, Patrick Macklem and Kent Roach (eds.), *The Security of Freedom: Essays on Canada's Anti-Terrorism Bill.* Toronto: University of Toronto Press.

Sheldrick, Byron. 2003. "Judicial Review and the Allocation of Health Care Resources in Canada and the United Kingdom." *Journal of Comparative Policy Analysis: Research and Practice* 5.

_____. 2000. "The Contradictions of Welfare to Work: Social Security Reform in Britain." *Studies in Political Economy* 62.

_____. 1998. "Judicial Review and Judicial Reticence: The Protection of Political Expression under the Common Law." *Journal of Civil Liberties* 3.

_____. 1995. "Law, Representation and Political Activism: Community-based Practice and the Mobilization of Legal Resources." *Canadian Journal of Law and Society* 10.

Sherman, Joan and Michael Gismondi. 1996. "Not Directly Affected: Using the Law to Close the Door on Environmentalists." *Journal of Canadian Studies* 31, 1.

Shields, John, and B. Mitchell Evans. 1998. *Shrinking the State: Globalization and Public Administration 'Reform.'* Halifax: Fernwood Publishing.

Sills, J.E. 1993. "SLAPPs (Strategic Lawsuits Against Public Participation): How Can the Legal System Eliminate their Appeal?" *Connecticut Law Review* 25, 2.

Slattery, Brian. 1987. "A Theory of the Charter." *Osgoode Hall Law Journal* 25.

Smart, Carol. 1989. *Feminism and the Power of Law.* London: Routledge.

Smith, Doug. 2002. *How to Tax a Billionaire.* Winnipeg: Arbeiter Ring Publishing.

Smith, Miriam. 2002. "Ghosts of the Judicial Committee of the Privy Council: Group Politics and Charter Litigation in Canadian Political Science." *Canadian Journal of Political Science* 35, 1.

_____. 1999. *Lesbian and Gay Rights in Canada: Social Movements and Equality Seeking, 1971–1995.* Toronto: University of Toronto Press.

Smith, Virginia Rose. 1998. "Canadians Ungagged: A Victory for Free Speech in *Daishowa v. Friends of the Lubicon.*" *Multinational Monitor* 19, 3.

Snow, David, and Robert Benford. 1988. "Ideology, Frame Resonance, and Participant Mobilization." In Bert Klandermans, Hanspeter Kriesi and Sidney Tarrow (eds.), *From Structure to Action: Comparing Social Movement Research across Cultures,* vol. 1. Greenwich: JAI Press.

Stanford, Jim. 2003. "'Third Way' Can't Survive Tony Blair." *Globe and Mail,* March 24.

Stuart, Don. 2002. "The Anti-Terrorism Bill C-36: An Unnecessary Law and Order Quick Fix that Permanently Stains the Canadian Criminal Justice

System." *National Journal of Constitutional Law* 14, 1.

Tarrow, Sydney. 1998. *Power in Movement: Social Movements and Contentious Politics*. 2nd edition. Cambridge: Cambridge University Press.

Thompson, E.P. 1975. *Whigs and Hunters: The Origins of the Black Act*. London: Allen Lane.

Thompson, Noel. 1984. *The People's Science: The Popular Political Economy of Exploitation and Crisis 1816–1834*. Cambridge: Cambridge University Press.

Tibbetts, Janice. 2002. "Lawyers Hope to Make Legal Aid a Charter Right." *National Post*. March 7.

Tollefson, Chris. 1996. "Strategic Lawsuits and Environmental Politics: *Daishowa Inc. v. Friends of the Lubicon*." *Journal of Canadian Studies* 31, 1.

Tremblay, Paul R. 1990. "Toward a Community-Based Ethic for Legal Services Practice." *UCLA Law Review* 37.

Trubek, Louise. 1991. "Critical Lawyering: Toward a New Public Interest Practice." *Boston University Public Interest Law Journal* 1, 49.

Vancouver Sun. 1992. "Law Firm Courted Controversy by Refusing Case." November 30: A6.

Waddams, S.M. 1997. *Introduction to the Study of Law*. Scarborough: Carswell.

Waddington, P.A.J. 1998. "Controlling Protest in Contemporary, Historical and Comparative Perspective." In Donatella della Porta and Herbert Retier (eds.), *Policing Protest: The Control of Mass Demonstrations in Western Democracies*. Minneapolis: University of Minnesota Press.

Wasik, Martin, and Richard Taylor. 1995. *Blackstone's Guide to the Criminal Justice and Public Order Act 1994*. London: Blackstone Press.

Watson, Sophie (ed.). 1990. *Playing the State: Australian Feminist Interventions (Questions for Feminism)*. London: Verso Books.

Whitaker, Reg. 1989. "Rights in a 'Free and Democratic' Society: Abortion." In David Shugarman and Reg Whitaker (eds.), *Federalism and Political Community: Essays in Honour of David Smiley*. Peterborough: Broadview Press.

Whyte, John. 1986. "Is the Private Sector Affected by the Charter?" In Lynn Smith (ed.), *Righting the Balance: Canada's New Equality Rights*. Saskatoon: Canadian Human Rights Reporter.

Winnipeg Free Press. 2003. "Gun-Registry Foes in PM's riding back accused." March 4.

Wristen, Karen. 1999. "Reaching into the Boardrooms." Available at <www.miningwatch.org/emcbc/publications/toolkit/5.htm>. Accessed on November 12, 2003.

CASES:

Andrews v. Law Society of British Columbia [1989] 1 Supreme Court Reports 143.

Anisminic Ltd. v. Foreign Compensation Commission [1969] 2 Appeal Cases 147 (House of Lords).

Brown v. Board of Education (1954) 347 U.S. 483.

Canadian Council of Churches v. The Queen [1992] 1 Supreme Court Reports 236.

Canadian Union of Public Employees, Local 963 v. New Brunswick Liquor Corp. [1979] 2 Supreme Court Reports 227 (SCC).

Clark v. Community for Creative Nonviolence (1984) 468 U.S. 288.

Daishowa Inc. v. Friends of the Lubicon (1998). 39 Ontario Reports (3d) 620..

Doucet-Boudreau v. Nova Scotia (Minister of Education) [2003] SCC 62 (Supreme Court of Canada).

Egan v. Canada [1995] 2 Supreme Court Reports 513.

Eldridge v. British Columbia [1997] 3 Supreme Court Reports 624.

Finlay v. Canada (Minister of Finance) [1986] 2 Supreme Court Reports 607.

Forsyth County, Georgia v. Nationalist Movement (1992) JIJ U.S. 123.

Gouriet v. Union of Post Office Workers [1978] Appeal Cases 435 (Eng. H.L).

Halpern et al. v. Attorney General of Ontario (June 10, 2003) Ontario Court of Appeal #C39172;C39174.

Kennett v. Health Sciences Centre (1991) 76 Manitoba Reports (2d) 47.

Lavigne v. Ontario Public Sector Employees Union [1991] 2 Supreme Court Reports 211.

McKinney v. The University of Guelph [1990] 3 Supreme Court Reports 229.

Metropolitan Life Insurance Co. v. International Union of Operating Engineers, Local 796 [1970] Supreme Court Reports 425.

Minister of Justice of Canada v. Borowski, [1981] 2 Supreme Court Reports 575.

Nova Scotia Board of Censors v. McNeil, [1976] 2 Supreme Court Reports 265.

Operation Dismantle v. The Queen [1985] 1 Supreme Court Reports 441.

Pezim v. British Columbia (Superintendant of Brokers) [1994] 2 Supreme Court Reports 557.

PSAC v. Canada [1987] 1 Supreme Court Reports 424.

R. v. Edward Books and Art [1986] 2 Supreme Court Reports 713.

R. v. Latimer [2001] 1 Supreme Court Reports 3.

R. v. Morgentaler [1988] 1 Supreme Court Reports 30.

R. v. Oakes [1986] 1 Supreme Court Reports 103.

R. v. Rodriguez [1993] 3 Supreme Court Reports 519.

Reference re Public Service Employment Relations Act (Alta.) [1987] 1 Supreme Court Reports 313.

Retail, Wholesale and Department Store Union, Local 580 v. Dolphin Delivery Ltd. [1986] 2 Supreme Court Reports 573.

Roe v. Wade (1973) 410 U.S. 113.

RWDSU v. Saskatchewan [1987] 1 Supreme Court Reports 460.

Save the Eaton's Building Coalition v. the City of Winnipeg and True North Partnership (August 10, 2001) <www.canlii.org/mb/cas/mbqb/2001/2001mbqb206.html>. Accessed on February 2, 2004.

Save the Eaton's Building Coalition v. the City of Winnipeg (June 4, 2002) <www.canlii.org/mb/cas/mbqb/2002/2002mbqb165.html>. Accessed on February 2, 2004.

Schacter v. Canada [1992] 2 Supreme Court Reports 679.

Scheidler v. National Organization for Women, Inc., U.S. Supreme Court, Feb. 16, 2003 available at <supct.law.cornell.edu/supct/html/01-1118.ZS.html>.

Seaboyer v. Gayme [1991] 2 Supreme Court Reports 577.

Shell Canada Products v. City of Vancouver (1994) 1 Dominion Law Reports (4th) 1.

Steel Co. aka Chicago Steel & Pickling Co. v. Citizens for a Better Environment (1998) 523 U.S. 83.

Thorson v. Attorney General of Canada [1975] 1 Supreme Court Reports 138.

Tremblay v. Daigle [1989] 2 Supreme Court Reports 530.

Valley Forge Christian College v. Americans United for Separation of Church and State, Inc., (1982) 454 U.S. 464.

Wedekind. v. Director of Income Maintenance Branch (Ont.) (1994),75 Ontario Appeal Cases 358.